Ladies of the Bedchamber

DENNIS FRIEDMAN

Ladies of the Bedchamber

The Role of the Royal Mistress

Peter Owen
LONDON & CHESTER SPRINGS

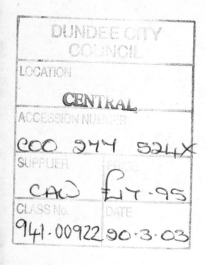
PETER OWEN PUBLISHERS

73 Kenway Road, London SW5 0RE

Peter Owen books are distributed in the USA by Dufour Editions Inc.,

Chester Springs, PA 19425-0007

First published in Great Britain 2003

© Dennis Friedman 2003

ISBN 0 7206 1160 1

A catalogue record for this book is available from
the British Library.

Printed in Croatia by
Zrinski SA

To my publisher, Peter Owen

Acknowledgements

Much has been written about the effects of extramarital sex on the sanctity of marriage. Social attitudes to adultery vary from strict adherence to religious imperatives, the acceptance that monogamy may be difficult to achieve and to recently published data that suggest that in some cases adultery may contribute to a healthy marriage. *Ladies of the Bedchamber* reflects on the misuse of power when reigning monarchs or their heirs allow themselves to be swayed from the path of duty by their sexual impulses.

I am grateful to Peter Owen for suggesting the work to me and to my wife, Rosemary Friedman, for her help and constant support during the writing of it. I thank my researcher Stephen Broomfield and my editor Bob Davenport for their unstinting efforts to ensure accuracy, as well as Douglas Matthews who did such a good job on the index. Many people willingly contributed family anecdotes. I am particularly grateful to Nicholas Moseley (Lord Ravensdale) for reminiscences about 'Fruity' Metcalfe, to the Hon. Julia Stonor for information about her great-great-aunt's life-long friendship with George V, to Penelope Craig for her views on her ancestor King Charles II, to Frank Hamilton for his recollections of the Duke of Windsor in America and to Dr Bernard Watkin for personal memorabilia relating to Edward VII.

I am also indebted to Oliver Everett, Keeper of the Royal Archives at Windsor, for permission to quote from royal letters and diaries that are in the public domain and, among others, to Collins for permission to quote from Philip Ziegler's *King Edward VIII*, to Aurum Press for permission to quote from Greg King's *Duchess of Windsor* and to Jonathan Cape for permission to quote from Alison Weir's *Henry VIII: King and Court*. Every effort has been made to ensure that there has been no infringement of copyright.

Thanks are also due to Professor Hugh Freeman, Bruce Robinson, Pauline Neville, Luisa Conde, Storm Kelly, Jacqueline Toff, Shirley Conran and Antonia Owen; also to the Press Association, the National Portrait Gallery and the Hulton Getty Picture Library for permission to reproduce photographs.

Contents

There can be no companion more agreeable than a loving mistress.
Jacques-Henri Bernardin de Saint-Pierre

Preface

'Lady of the bedchamber' is generally the title given a sovereign's female attendant. But some ladies of the bedchamber have warmed the beds of reigning British monarchs or their heirs in more intimate ways. In so doing, they not only have boosted royal egos and affected the morals of the country but in some cases have altered the course of history. The combination of sexual potency and constitutional power can produce an aphrodisiac effect which, like that of mood-enhancing drugs, has constantly to be topped up. In these cases preoccupation with their sexual needs has diverted sovereigns and their heirs not only from family responsibilities but from affairs of state.

A mistress, royal or otherwise, does not usually choose her role. She may find herself in such a relationship for a number of reasons: a desire to be envied by other women for the power bestowed by her consort; a compulsive need to procreate; a fear of intimacy and an inability to cope with marital commitment; envy of other women and the desire to steal their men. What does the royal mistress have to gain from her association with kings and princes? Is sexual power, like sexually transmitted disease, contagious? Does power by proxy – 'I've danced with a man who danced with a girl who danced with the Prince of Wales' – enhance the lives of those who wield it or prove socially destructive? Some men, uncertain of their potency – whether sexual, social, political or constitutional – regard a mistress as a status symbol and think that she can be worn on the arm like an expensive watch. Such men are in need of constant reassurance, and if they change their women's lives it is seldom for the better.

That an illicit liaison will lead to marriage is the ultimate hope of many mistresses. Others are satisfied with the empowerment that their relationships (often with older men) provide: Monica Lewinsky with Bill Clinton; Marilyn Monroe with John F. Kennedy; Christine Keeler with John Profumo. Grandiose men and tyrannical leaders demean their mistresses, whom they use only to satisfy their demanding sex drives: examples are Soviet secret-police chief Lavrenti Beria and his passion for schoolgirls, Mao Tse-tung and his predilection for flight attendants, Henry VIII and his unrelenting search for a woman to provide him with male heirs.

A mistress, like many other ill-gotten gains, is often a closely guarded secret. To bring the relationship out into the open would be to deprive it of the reason for its existence in the first place; namely the heightened sexual arousal generated by a forbidden relationship which is often frowned upon by society and in conflict with the marriage contract solemnly agreed to by one or both partners in the affair. The mistress has no rights in law, and breach of promise is no longer on the statute book. There is no one to whom a 'kept' woman can appeal for protection of her interests, no ombudsman to speak up for her. Her acceptance of her role ensures that she is a paid-up member of the sexual secret service and is thereby effectively served with a gagging order by her married controller.

Before the twentieth century, many wives were relieved when their husbands did not 'bother' them, for when they did, owing to the lack of reliable contraception, the result was often serial and frequently life-threatening pregnancies. They were therefore content to turn a blind eye to male sexual philanderings. Princess Alexandra certainly experienced the infidelities of her husband, later King Edward VII, as a welcome relief from child-bearing.

Ladies of the Bedchamber reveals how sex addiction has cast its shadow over the royal family from the late Middle Ages to the end of the twentieth century. This addiction has threaded its way through the thousand years of the British monarchy to the present day via the infidelities of Henry VIII (with their often macabre outcome), via James II, who expected his mistresses to be thin; via Edward VII, who expected his mistresses to be married; and via Edward VIII, who expected his mistresses to understand him.

Attention is focused on the psychological imperatives of the sexual indiscretions of a long line of monarchs and also those of their mistresses, from Nell Gwyn to Lily Langtry and Sarah Bernhardt, and from the *grande dame* of mistresses, Wallis Simpson – who may unwittingly have saved Great Britain from Nazi domination – to Camilla Parker Bowles.

Those not in its grip acknowledge the *coup de foudre* as a short-lived illusion. Falling in love represents a wish to remedy the unsatisfactory aspects of the earlier love-affair that each of the partners will have had with a mother. The behaviour of newborn infants suggests that a baby is convinced that his (or her) mother exists only for him and that the boundaries of her breast are the boundary of his world. The infant is in love with the mother who comforts him when he cries and feeds him when he is hungry, and he expects his mother to be in love with him. If she does her job properly she will instil faithfulness into her child. If she does not, her child, if male, will later punish other women – often married women with children – for her failings and will play the 'love them and leave them' game. Or, if the child is female, as an adult she will dislike other women and also herself. She may envy others their happiness and try to rob them of their loving partners.

This first love-affair with the mother is thus a vital one. If it has provided the infant with self-esteem and a sense of self-worth, there will be no need to seek these later. As adults, men and women will be content to exchange care, compassion and concern with a loving partner. If the first love-affair has been unsatisfactory, however, men will be condemned to spend their lives looking for – and even paying for – that which should have been theirs as of right, while women, often equally promiscuous, will use sex to captivate men. Having been denied their expectations and embarrassed by the need to re-enact earlier intimacies, both men and women will be either angry or depressed. A philandering man will set out to make another conquest, to fight a battle that would have been unnecessary had he bonded with his mother in the first place. A promiscuous woman will do the same. Later the person will fall in love with 'parent figures' and often punish them for the inadequacies of his or her own parents.

Men whose mothers, or surrogate mothers, have been less than attentive will either abuse women that they marry or live with or seek compensation from women other than their partners. Their testosterone-driven urge to succeed, their need for approval, and their drive for the power that a loving mother could have provided will fuel their extramarital affairs.

Mothers, connected by same-sex understanding, bond more easily with their female infants, with whom they are more likely to feel at one. It could be some time before a baby girl realizes that there is also a man in her life. If for any reason this man should disappear, as an adult she may superimpose his image upon other males, deluding herself that she has found his archetype.

Though a woman's failed primary love-affair is more likely to have been with her father rather than her mother, when she later falls in love as an adult she will suffer from the same delusions as a man, and the familiar 'eyes across a crowded room' phenomenon may give rise to the mistaken belief that she has stumbled upon her 'other half'.

Women, in general, do not attempt to make conquests. The female sex hormone encourages them to use more sensitive tactics. A woman who believes that she has never been loved for herself will instead employ seduction. She will use her charms and erotic signals to 'get round' a man in the hope that he will find her irresistible.

Victims of childhood neglect are often unable to cope with intimacy. Their later commitments will provoke a passionate and inevitably recurring need for love, which is doomed to be followed by rejection and disappointment. That this is as true for the royal family as for other families the following chapters will demonstrate.

Henry VIII

Liaisons Dangereuses

Henry VIII grew up in a century of immortals. Five hundred years later his name is as familiar as that of Titian, Tintoretto, Botticelli, Leonardo da Vinci, Michelangelo, Copernicus, Calvin, Christopher Columbus or Vasco da Gama. He is famed, however, not for his creative achievements but for his continued attempts to produce a healthy male heir – attempts which transformed him from a prodigal son into a psychopathic murderer.

Henry was born in Greenwich Palace on 28 June 1491. As a child he was prone to temper tantrums and could only with difficulty be soothed by his attendants. He loved food, and was comforted by it. But he could not tolerate frustration, wanted immediate gratification and became angry if made to wait for anything – hardly surprising given that it took ten years for any member of his family to show the slightest interest in him.

Henry was the second son of King Henry VII, who had devoted much of his life to a struggle to bring peace and prosperity to an embattled England. Having spent the reign of Edward IV in exile in Brittany, Henry VII had eventually come to the throne in 1485 after killing his Yorkist predecessor, Richard III, at the Battle of Bosworth Field. He arranged for Richard's drawn and quartered body to be paraded through the streets of Leicester as proof that the House of York had been similarly torn apart. Henry VII earned the gratitude of his people by ending the Wars of the Roses, uniting the Houses of Lancaster and York and founding the Tudor dynasty

Henry VII had survived against a background of war. A gloomy introvert, secretive, uncommunicative and paranoid – seeing danger everywhere and often making pre-emptive strikes on targets that existed only in his imagination – his main concern was the preservation of the House of Tudor, and his achievement was to hand on the makings of a modern state to his heirs. It would have been logical for him to involve himself in his children's upbringing, but he had time for neither his two sons, Arthur and Henry, nor his two daughters, Margaret and Mary. His main concern was that Prince Arthur, the Prince of Wales, be groomed to inherit the throne. His children could address him only on the rare occasions when he permitted them to do so.

Their mother, Elizabeth of York, was the daughter of King Edward IV; Henry VII had married her as part of a deal for ending the war between Lancaster and York. Certainly more kind-hearted than her disagreeable husband, Elizabeth was, however, worn out by her seven pregnancies and too much in love with her husband to find time to care for the needs of her children.

Prince Henry's future as a major player on the world stage became apparent only when, in April 1502, his fragile elder brother died from tuberculosis at the age of fifteen, having been married for less than a year to Catherine of Aragon, daughter of King Ferdinand II and Queen Isabella of Spain. Henry VII had hoped that by arranging for Arthur to marry Catherine he would be retaining King Ferdinand as a powerful ally in his ongoing problems with France.

Given his lack of emotional interest in his children, Henry VII was less distressed by the death of his eldest son than by the possible loss of his recently acquired Spanish ally. He knew that he had a moral obligation to return Catherine's only partially paid dowry to her parents, but he was always reluctant to give up anything he had acquired. He decided to hold on to the money and keep Catherine a virtual prisoner in England with the intention of marrying her off to his second son, Henry, if the canon law that forbade a man to marry his brother's widow could be circumvented and if a more advantageous match did not present itself. Catherine was not consulted about this, but she would in any case have been in no position to object. She had arrived – not yet sixteen – a year earlier after a prolonged sea voyage from Corunna, with her ladies-in-waiting, her confessor and her servants. The beautiful Spanish princess, welcomed by cheering crowds as she travelled from Plymouth to London, spoke no English. As Arthur spoke no Spanish, she and her ever-coughing spouse communicated haltingly in

Latin (and then only with a bishop translating). She missed her parents, hated the weather and, after Arthur's death, resented having to wait in the wings for the end of her father-in-law's hopes of a still better marriage for his heir. Despite being six years older than Prince Henry, Catherine felt that any husband must be better than her previous one, whose poor health and need to be cared for had made him a burden.

Catherine, in fact, was attracted to Henry. His appearance suggested a self-sufficiency that she only later came to realize concealed an insatiable desire for love and approval. And Henry was pleased to be betrothed to Catherine. She was warm and motherly, and he had liked her from the day she had arrived from Spain to marry his brother.

But, to Henry VII's annoyance, Pope Julius II ruled that Catherine could marry Henry only if her marriage to Arthur had not been consummated. An obliging lady-in-waiting, called upon to examine the girl, confirmed that the bride was still a virgin. This pleased the devious King, though he knew that on the morning after Arthur's wedding his exhausted but triumphant older son had ordered Sir Anthony Willoughby, one of his attendants, to 'bring me a cup of ale, for I have been this night in the midst of Spain'. The King chose to accept the testament of the Bishop of Ely, who claimed that Catherine had often told him that she had never 'carnally known' Prince Arthur. Prince Henry, still a few days short of his twelfth birthday, was immediately betrothed to the seventeen-year-old widow and was obliged to accept the awesome responsibility of a role on which he had not been consulted and about which his feelings were mixed.

Though sad at the loss of his nursery playmate, Henry could not help feeling angry with his brother. Arthur had burdened him with a liability that effectively ended his childhood and threw him into a dynastic whirlpool in which the perpetuation of the House of Tudor, which could be secured only by the birth of a male heir, was paramount. Female children were of no interest. They were disinherited not by the King but by their gender. England had as yet never had a female sovereign, and Henry would have been horrified had he known that, of his three legitimate children, two of them – first Mary and then Elizabeth – would one day reign over a country whose destiny, his grandiosity told him, belonged solely to his male heirs.

Following the death of his brother, the ten-year-old Henry, suddenly burdened with responsibility, had been obliged to give up all pretence to scholarship in order to concentrate on his destiny. Character traits that were later to become a feature of his personality – such as extravagance of mood, lack of concern for the feelings of others, intolerance of criticism, theatricality and self-dramatization – began to surface as he waited impatiently for his father to die so that he could inherit the throne and further his ambition to become the most powerful man in Christendom. Henry was in awe of his father and admired and envied his achievements. As a young man he had already resolved to go one better by transforming Christian England into a world power, with himself as its omnipotent head. Such grandiose ambition was later realized only by usurping the vicarious power of the Pope, God's vicar on earth, in order to secure a divorce which the Catholic Church refused him, contributing to disunity among Christians which five hundred years later the Church is still trying to resolve.

Whatever distress Henry's father may have felt about the loss of the sickly Prince Arthur was tempered by his confidence in his ruggedly healthy second son, and he looked forward to the benefits that would ensue for the country when Henry inherited the throne. He congratulated himself on having the virility required to produce an heir and a spare.

When his wife died in childbirth ten months after Arthur's death, in February 1503, he was devastated, for, despite the arranged marriage, he had come to love Elizabeth and to depend on her. Unlike many husbands of the time, Henry had been faithful to his wife, and in return she had brought tranquillity to his life after his years of exile. Henry had fought Richard of York both for England and for Elizabeth. He never recovered from his wife's death, and in his depressed state he became even less available to his adolescent second son. The Spanish envoy complained that Prince Henry 'was locked away like a woman' for his own protection, since his father could not afford to lose an heir who, though barely past puberty, already looked every inch a king.

Worn out by intrigue and the fear of attempts on his life by Yorkist claimants to the throne, Henry VII died in 1509, leaving the throne to his seventeen-year-old son. Thirteen days later Prince Henry married his sister-

in-law, Catherine of Aragon, and subsequently underwent a double coronation in Westminster Abbey.

As a baby, Prince Henry had been pink, beautiful and healthy – a miniature, blue-eyed English aristocrat. As a fully grown adult he was tall,
red-headed, good-looking and athletic. After he came to the throne he was
described as 'the handsomest sovereign in Christendom [with] a round face
so beautiful it would become a pretty woman'. Portrait painters such as
Hans Holbein were deliberately encouraged to exaggerate the magnificence
and power of his image.

Henry was admired not only for his appearance but also for his artistic
abilities. During the lifetime of his brother he had been intended for the
archbishopric of Canterbury and had received a good education. As an adolescent he was an accomplished lute and harpsichord player, wrote masses,
madrigals and popular ballads and had a fine singing voice. He was said to
be much impressed by the concept of courtly love and was easily offended by
lewd talk. (Such squeamishness is not uncommon in the amoral, and Henry
shared this hypocrisy with Adolf Hitler, another tyrant, who was always correct with his 'friend' Eva Braun.) Henry once angrily dismissed Sir Andrew
Flammock from his presence for having completed a verse in lewd language.
Henry had challenged Flammock to complete the doggerel:

> Within this tower
> There lieth a flower
> That hath my heart . . .

Flammock had suggested:

> Within this hour
> She pissed full sour
> And let a fart.

He knew French, Spanish and some Italian and had a good knowledge
of Latin. But, though he began his early adult life in the vanguard of the arts,
he is remembered not for his intellect nor for his creative potential but as a

six times married, sexually promiscuous psychopath, responsible for the execution of two of his wives and some 80,000 of his subjects.

In 1491, the year in which Henry was born, life was cheap. Ninety per cent of the population died from disease or violence before they reached the age of forty. The infant mortality rate was incalculable, and only three of King Henry VIII's nineteen or so children (legitimate or otherwise) survived into adulthood. Was Henry merely a product of his time and was social hardship the only backdrop to his reign, or did the once golden boy take a wrong turning as the consequence of bad parenting? Was his compulsive womanizing a reflection of his need for the attention and approval he was denied as a child, or were his women willing agents of their own destruction because they could not deny themselves the life-enhancing aphrodisiac effect of sexual congress with a king?

'Our time is spent in continual festival,' declared Catherine soon after her marriage. She was carried away by Henry's love for her, as was he by hers for him. Henry and his Queen seemed to be made for one another. Catherine, a political pawn sent by her parents from Spain over seven years earlier for an uncertain life in England with a man neither she nor they had ever met, had at last found someone to love her. Equally, Henry had found in Catherine a joyous companion who would always be by his side and dancing to his tune. Leaving, as he thought, the tyranny of his childhood behind him, two weeks before he celebrated his eighteen birthday he was finally a free man.

Unfortunately for Henry this freedom was little more than an illusion. Increasingly embittered by an upbringing in which the need to focus entirely on the importance of his royal inheritance had denied him his wish to study the arts, he embarked on a career to redress its wrongs.

Henry had been brought up to believe that it was his duty to perpetuate the Tudor monarchy. That much he owed his seldom available and therefore much needed father. His compulsive urge to please his father by producing a male heir forced him to regard his wives primarily as reproductive vehicles.

Catherine's first four children were to die at or soon after birth between 1510 and 1514. Her serial pregnancies, the result of her vain efforts to bear the King a son, deprived her husband of sex. Though at the time it may have been customary for sexual activity to cease during pregnancy, Henry, having found in his marriage some relief for his pent-up passions (love for his wife and hate for his parents), was incapable of postponing his emotional needs.

During Catherine's second pregnancy, in 1510, Lady Anne Hastings – the sister of the Duke of Buckingham and the wife of Sir George Hastings (later the Earl of Huntingdon) – was offered the dubious privilege of becoming the first of Henry's mistresses. She did not hesitate. The heady cocktail of sex with a king and a man as young and good-looking as Henry was too good to pass up. Catherine was distressed by Henry's infidelity, the Duke of Buckingham was enraged by it, and the embarrassed twenty-year-old Henry (whose conscience had not as yet entirely abandoned him) denied it.

Anne Hastings and her older sister, Elizabeth, were ladies-in-waiting to the Queen. Anne's relationship with Henry arose out of a minor dispute with her sister as to which one of them would 'comfort' the King during his wife's pregnancy. Because of their closeness to Catherine, both Anne and Elizabeth (Henry's second cousins) were only too well aware of his sexual needs. The affair between Anne and Henry seemed at the time to be of as little importance as the dispute between the two sisters. Anne Hastings would have had no difficulty in convincing herself that she was only doing her duty to her mistress, though she recognized that she was also promoting her own interests.

Henry's affair with Anne was the first time that he had taken a serious interest in a woman outside his marriage, and he could not have chosen a woman more sociably acceptable. Anne Hastings had impeccable connections. She was born Anne Stafford at Penshurst Castle, in Kent, the grandest of the estates of the Stafford family, whose first-born sons were dukes of Buckingham. Her father, Henry Stafford, the 2nd Duke of Buckingham, was descended from the youngest son of King Edward IV and had in 1483 been executed for treason by Richard III. Anne and Elizabeth were both sisters of the 3rd Duke of Buckingham, who himself had a weak claim to the throne. Though he was the premier peer of the realm, his relationship with Henry had never been close. Elizabeth was the wife of Robert Ratcliffe, Lord Fitzwalter, and the aunt by marriage of Anne Boleyn.

Luis Caroz, the Spanish ambassador, wrote of Henry's affair with Anne Hastings in a letter dated 28 May 1510: 'What lately has happened is that two sisters of the Duke of Buckingham, both married, lived in the Palace.

One of them is the favourite of the Queen and the other, it is said, is much liked by the King who went after her.' He added, however, that

> Another version [has it] that the love intrigues were not of the King, but of a young man, his favourite, by the name of [Sir William] Compton [the King's Groom of the Stool], who carried on the love intrigue, as it is said, for the King, and that is the more credible version, as the King has shown great displeasure at what I am going to tell.
>
> The favourite of the Queen has been very anxious in the matter of her sister, and has joined herself with the Duke her brother, with her husband and her sister's husband in order to consult on what should be done. The consequences [were] that, whilst the Duke was in the private apartments of his sister, who was suspected with the King, Compton came there to talk with her, saw the Duke, who intercepted him, quarrelled with him, and the end of it was that he was severely reproached in many very hard words. The King was so offended at this that he reprimanded the Duke angrily. The same night, the Duke left the palace and did not return for some days. At the same time, the husband of that lady went away, carried her off, and placed her in a convent sixty miles from here, that no one might see her.
>
> The King, having understood that all this proceeded from the sister who is the favourite of the Queen, the day after the one was gone turned the other out of the palace, and her husband with her. Believing that there were other women in the employment of the favourite such as go about the palace insidiously spying out every unwatched movement in order to tell the Queen, the King would have liked to turn all of them out, only that it has appeared to him too great a scandal. Afterwards, almost all the court knew that the Queen had been vexed with the King, and the King with her, and thus the storm went on between them. The Queen by no means conceals her ill-will towards Compton, and the King is very sorry for it.

Sir William Compton is known to have lived in an adulterous relationship with Lady Hastings. He later founded a chantry at Compton Wynyates in Warwickshire, where prayers were said for her soul (and presumably Henry's) and for the souls of members of his own family. However, when Caroz tried to lecture Fra Diego Fernandez (the Queen's confessor) on the Queen's responsibilities to Spain and to England – to produce an heir – he was told by Fernandez that he had got the whole story wrong.

There was never a time in Henry's adult life when a woman was not at his side or in his bed. Life without them was not worth living. This should not suggest that the King actually liked women, however. It was more likely that he hated them. His multiple sexual conquests were partly a reflection of his narcissistic personality and partly the result of a fruitless search for the love denied him as a child. Henry had never bonded with his mother, and in his adult life this was reflected in an angry and untiring search for his maternal entitlement from other women (many of them mothers and more often than not in good relationships with their partners). He acted out his hostility by professing fidelity and practising infidelity and by turning his back on one woman after another in his search for the unconditional love that had been denied to him.

In fact women loved him and competed with one another to possess him. They were captivated by his seductive behaviour – unaware that anyone who needs to get round another person in order to be loved has little or no self-esteem. Believing, in tune with the times, that women were born to suffer, perhaps Henry's women thought little of the cost to them of his 'love'. What was certain was that his power over them arose not from inner strength but from his position. In his compulsive quest for a mother figure, he drove one woman after another into a state of motherhood that sometimes killed them.

Obsessed by mothers, Henry heartily disliked fathers. His affairs with married women momentarily satisfied his own maternal needs, and their husbands (the fathers) usually acquiesced without a struggle.

While promiscuity came easily to him – and was mainly responsible for the sexually transmitted diseases suffered by his wives – he could not tolerate it in others. The defence of his ego, the defence of his realm and the provision of a male heir were his priorities. Henry constantly needed to be reassured of his potency. Fertility, then as now, was considered proof of virility. In the absence of such proof, Henry relied on his sword to demonstrate his power over other men. Enemies – whether real or imagined – were ruthlessly eliminated. Greatness might have been thrust upon him, but having acquired it he had no intention of giving it up. If his head was uneasy beneath the crown, the weight of the headache was a constant reminder of his addiction to grandiosity. He worked for it, fought for it and – when it was not on offer – stole it, if not on the battlefield then in the bedroom.

Once on the throne, despite opportunity and personal talent, Henry gradually lost interest in the cultural renaissance of the times. His long-suppressed emotional needs produced a hunger for sex and power so insatiable that he had difficulty in concentrating on any political issues of the day that did not affect him personally. Essentially self-conscious, with low self-esteem and with increasing doubts about his inability to produce a male heir, he became preoccupied with proving both to himself and to others that he was a giant among men. In 1513 he invaded France and, with the help of 2,000 Austrian mercenaries, won the Battle of the Spurs. He relied on women to reassure him of his sexual potency and on the execution of his rivals and the defeat of the French in the Hundred Years War to reassure him of his political power.

Henry VIII's second extramarital affair was as opportunistic as the first. On this occasion it was not with a lady-in-waiting but with a teacher of the French language. Jane Popincourt had come to England from France to act as a tutor to Henry's sisters. She was older and more discreet than Anne Hastings – so discreet, in fact, that very little is known about her.

Henry's third mistress, however, the eighteen-year-old Elizabeth Blount, made a greater impression on him, and in 1518 he claimed to be 'much in love' with her. She had come to court as a mature-looking thirteen-year-old maid of honour to Catherine of Aragon, and, despite her youth, she was thought to have already been the lover of the Duke of Suffolk, a close friend of the King.

When members of the royal household complained about the amorous intrigues of Catherine's confessor, Fra Diego Fernandez, he was summoned before the King. When he responded to the accusations about his own behaviour with comments about the Queen being badly used by Henry, this was probably a reference to the King's involvement with Elizabeth Blount. Fortunately for Fra Diego, Henry had not yet reached the stage in his career when the penalty for disagreeing with him was execution. The indiscreet priest was merely sent back to Spain.

Elizabeth Blount, an accomplished dancer and singer, was both high-spirited and energetic – much as Catherine had been when Henry married her. Even when Elizabeth was middle-aged, and had born seven children by three lovers or husbands, a visitor to her house remarked that he 'had very good cheer with her'.

Henry's infatuation with Elizabeth probably began at Christmas 1514, when in a masque at a Christmas pageant at Greenwich she played one of the Four Ladies of Savoy 'rescued from danger' by the Four Knights of Portugal, one of whom was played by Henry. When the identities of the dancers were revealed, Elizabeth thanked Henry for 'her goodly pastime and kissed him'.

By the time the affair was at its height, between 1515 and 1516, Catherine was again pregnant – this time with Mary. Once again Henry had sought sexual comfort outside the marriage, having convinced himself that infidelity during a wife's pregnancy was both acceptable and unexceptional among members of his court. His growing resentment at Catherine's failure to provide him with a male heir led him to become quite open about his affair with Elizabeth Blount. Unlike his wife, his mistress not only became pregnant but produced the boy for which the King had been waiting. Henry was overjoyed. His virility was no longer in doubt, and the boy was christened Henry Fitzroy. (Fitzroy, meaning 'son of the King', was the name appropriately given to illegitimate royal sons.)

Henry was now in dispute with his wife and took pleasure in humiliating her by organizing joyous celebrations for the birth of the son upon whom he doted and by having the boy brought up at court. Elizabeth Blount was openly accepted as 'the Mother of the King's Son'. By the time he was six Henry Fitzroy had been granted the title of Duke of Richmond and Somerset and at ten was appointed Lord Lieutenant of Ireland. His father also provided him with a home in Yorkshire, with 250 servants, that was as grand as any of the royal palaces. Despite all this, the King's vision did not extend to legitimizing his son as his rightful heir. Had he done so, his treatment of his wives as reproductive factories would never have been necessary.

Henry Fitzroy was to die in July 1536 at the early age of seventeen from tuberculosis, two months after witnessing Anne Boleyn's death on the scaffold. His birth had taken place in 1519 – nine years after Catherine had first failed to produce a son for the King – at a house in Blackmore in Essex known as Jericho (since it abutted the River Can, which was referred to locally as the River Jordan). The house had a reputation as being a trysting place where Henry had previously met Elizabeth Blount and others in privacy and 'where the King's Highness have his privy chamber and inward lodgings reserved secret, at the pleasure of His Grace, without repair of any great multitude'. In 1527 the house was given to Cardinal Thomas Wolsey, known by his enemies as 'the King's Bawd', because of his activities as a procurer of young women for Henry while still a prince and also for finding a husband for Elizabeth when the affair was over. Such gratitude did not come easily to Henry. He had not learned it from his parents. There was nothing in their behaviour towards him that taught him to be appreciative.

At the end of an affair Henry did not look back. He was ready to move on. By providing him with a son, Elizabeth Blount had fulfilled the role that the King had demanded of her. What better (and more cynical) way of disposing of her than by arranging for her marriage to someone else? Wolsey – not only a procurer of women but also a disposer of them – was called in. For Elizabeth he chose one of his wards, Gilbert Tallboys (or Tailboys). As Tallboys's father, Lord Kyme, was mentally incapable of managing his own affairs, his estates were held in trust by the Crown and he himself was placed in the custody of the Duke of Norfolk. Land belonging to him in Lincolnshire and Somerset was released to Gilbert Tallboys on his marriage to Elizabeth, who was in addition awarded a dowry by Parliament. Bribery paid off for her. Elizabeth had three children by Tallboys, and after her husband's death in 1530 (when he was MP for Lincoln and its sheriff) she turned down a proposal from Lord Leonard Grey and instead chose to become the wife of the 9th Baron Clinton (Edward Fiennes de Clinton), who was fourteen years her junior. She bore him three daughters, and in 1539, at the age of forty, died happy in the knowledge that she had lived her life to the full.

Catherine was disgusted by Henry's decision to have his illegitimate son should be brought up at court, and for the first time she rebelled against his blatant taunting of her failure to produce a male heir. The King's renowned temper now erupted, and, turning his back on his once loyal wife, he invited one woman after another to his bedchamber, even when Catherine was not encumbered by pregnancy.

Henry's next mistress was Mary Boleyn. Her mother was the former Elizabeth Howard, a member of the Queen's household by virtue of her birth-rank. She was the daughter of the 2nd Duke of Norfolk, the Earl Marshal of England, and her father had close links with Henry since he had been Squire of the Body at the funeral of Henry VII. Rumour had it that the ever voracious Henry had even seduced Elizabeth Howard. George Throckmorton, a brave but obviously foolhardy Member of Parliament, challenged the King on this issue. Henry soon put his mind at rest: 'Never with the mother' was his perhaps over-precise reply.

Mary's father, Sir Thomas Boleyn, was much admired by the King, and in 1523 Henry acquired two ships from him, the *Anne Boleyn* and the *Mary Boleyn*. (It is sometimes thought that the King gave the ships these names, but they were already so called when he acquired them.) Thomas Boleyn was the son of a London merchant but had bettered himself by marrying into the noble Howard family. Slightly younger than the King and an expert jouster and linguist, he was a joint constable of Norwich Castle and sheriff of Kent. As English ambassador to France in 1519–20, Sir Thomas was responsible for administration at the summit meeting between Henry and François I of France at the Field of Cloth of Gold. He was described as 'outstandingly learned' by Erasmus, from whom he commissioned works. He was industrious and dogged but had problems with giving anything of himself to his children or any of his money to those who depended on him. Because he himself managed to live on a tiny income, he expected everyone else to do the same. He boasted that 'when I married I had only £50 a year to live on for me and my wife so long as my father lived, and yet she brought me a child every year'. He was created Viscount Rochford in 1525, probably as a gift from the King's sister Mary.

The affair between the King and Mary Boleyn began almost immediately after she married William Carey, gentleman of the King's household, in February 1520. There were two children of the marriage, Catherine and Henry. Though Mary's son, Henry, resembled the King in looks and a nun pointed him out to the local vicar as the King's bastard, Henry VIII never recognized him as he recognized Henry Fitzroy. Henry Carey would later claim that he was 'our sovereign lord the King's son', but his father was almost certainly William Carey. The King had convinced himself that the affair with Mary was over well before the boy was conceived and had no wish to be involved in unnecessary publicity.

Mary's husband knew about her affair with the King, but it was conducted with tact and discretion, and he thought it wise to ignore it. He realized that there was nothing to be gained and everything to be lost (including his head) by challenging the King. In a generous moment, Henry rewarded William Carey for his tact by creating him Keeper of the Palace at Greenwich in 1526, and when Mary was left in straitened circumstances after the early death of her husband, from the plague in 1528, Henry granted her an annual pension of £100 (worth around £30,000 today) and commanded her father to look after her. Henry had refused her requests for financial help in the past, and her pension was probably more to impress her older sister, Anne, than to assuage any minimal feelings of guilt he may have had.

Despite ten years of pregnancies, Catherine had managed to produce only one live daughter. She reluctantly accepted that Henry must either establish a liaison with a woman at court or divorce her and remarry. She prepared herself for the inevitable.

It is unlikely that Henry would have remained married to Catherine even had she not worn herself out trying to give him a son. Unable to prevent her four sons either from dying at birth or being stillborn, Catherine was now approaching forty and was no longer attractive. In 1527 Henry set about obtaining a divorce. Calling upon religious belief – which, despite his fondness for ritual, he observed mainly in the breach – he decided that Catherine was not after all his lawful wife, because he had disregarded the injunction of Leviticus 18.16: 'Thou shalt not uncover the nakedness of thy brother's wife.' He chose to ignore Leviticus 20.10: 'And the man that committeth adultery with another man's wife, even he that committeth adultery with his neighbour's wife, the adulterer and the adulteress shall surely be put to death.' Thomas Cromwell, Cardinal Wolsey's Secretary, advised Henry to instruct Wolsey to arrange a divorce, on the grounds that the marriage to Catherine was contrary to God's wishes. Henry, a fundamentalist when it suited him, told Wolsey that what it said in the Bible must be true.

Despite his best efforts between 1528 and 1530, Wolsey failed to achieve a satisfactory verdict from Rome. Pope Clement said that his predecessor, Julius II, had granted Henry a dispensation to marry Catherine, and it was not possible for the Church of Rome to reverse another Pope's decision. Henry was so infuriated by Wolsey's failure to obtain what he wanted that he ordered him to be brought to London to face trial. Had he not died on the way to the Tower of London, the Cardinal would have been impeached and executed for treason.

Henry, thwarted by a bigotry he easily identified in others but never in himself, had had enough. England, he said, would no longer be ruled from Rome. Appointing himself the first head of the Church of England, in 1531, he appointed the compliant Thomas Cranmer as Archbishop of Canterbury.

Cranmer's first task was to declare Henry's marriage to Catherine null and void. Rid of his wife, who had failed in her mothering role, and rid of Il Papa – the Pope, the authoritarian father who had also failed him – Henry split the Christian Church in England down the middle in the interest of his sexual needs. Nearly five hundred years later, despite paying lip-service to liberal ecumenism, the two branches of Christianity continue to be divided by strife in at least one corner of the British Isles, and heirs to the throne of Great Britain are still forbidden to marry Catholics, on pain of losing their right of succession.

The Italian politician Niccolò Machiavelli, who in his native Florence had never objected to morally questionable methods being used in the interests of the state, described Henry VIII at this time as 'rich, ferocious and greedy for power'. The excitement of being not only the most powerful man in England but also the most popular seemed temporarily to dissipate some of the anger left over from the King's emotionally deprived upbringing.

Henry's affair with Mary Boleyn did not remain a secret for long. In

1527, having set his mind on divorcing Catherine, he had asked the Pope to rule on the possibility of his then marrying Mary's sister Anne. This was an ecclesiastical necessity, because Henry was going against the Church's rule on consanguinity through having had a sexual relationship with Mary; marriage to Anne would normally count as an unacceptable degree of affinity.

Anne was probably born in or around 1500 at Blickling Hall, Norfolk. Like most girls of her time she was uneducated, though able to read and write. Henry's relationship with her did not follow the usual pattern. Despite the vigour of his wooing, which no previous woman had been able to resist, it was some time before Anne gave any sign that she was interested in becoming his Queen.

Unlike her sister, Anne claimed to be serious and pious – though she had already had at least two lovers. She played hard to get, knowing only too well what was likely to happen to Henry's mistresses. She told him bluntly and in so many words that if he wanted sex with her he would have to marry her. She claimed hypocritically that 'I would rather lose my life than my honesty.' Despite her earlier protestations to the contrary, however, when she was sufficiently reassured that Henry's intentions towards her were 'honourable' she agreed to take over her sister's role as his mistress. She was pregnant shortly before the marriage but presented Henry not with a much wanted son, but with a beautiful red-haired daughter – Elizabeth, later to become Queen Elizabeth I.

The wedding took place in January 1533 with little or no publicity. Anne was deeply distressed that for the most part the public did not care for her. She was considered an upstart, her grandfather had been in trade, and many thought her insufficiently high class to be their Queen. Though she was charitable, generous and musical and wrote poetry, none of this increased her popularity with her subjects or with the King. She could not help noticing that, despite the vagaries of her husband's private life, the public continued to react to him as if he were still a seventeen-year-old golden boy.

By the end of 1534, having not yet succeeded in her duty to produce a son, Anne was becoming increasingly sensitive on this issue. With her position with her husband worsening, she resented her sister Mary's highlighting of her inadequacies by her sudden appearance at court remarried and pregnant. Incensed by what she considered Mary's gloating emphasis on her failure and having for some time been subject to attacks of uncontrollable rage, Anne persuaded Henry to cut off her sister's allowance and banish both Mary and her husband from court.

Increasingly stressed by the pressures put upon her to produce an heir, Anne had begun to irritate the King. He had no patience with her low mood and constant tiredness and had no understanding of what would today be recognized as clinical depression. He had not experienced it, therefore it did not exist. His personality was such that he provoked psychological symptoms in those around him but never in himself

Three months after her allowance was withdrawn, Mary wrote to Thomas Cromwell – now a rising man – and asked him to act as an intermediary in trying to effect a reconciliation with her sister, presumably so that her pension might be restored. She managed to do it in terms that further inflamed Anne's temper: 'for well I might a'had a greater man of birth but I assure you I could never a'had one that loved me so well. I had rather beg my bread with him than be the greatest Queen christened.' Her new husband, William Stafford, was a man of very modest fortune and social standing, though a distant cousin of the Duke of Buckingham. Mary, poor but none the less happy, spent the rest of her days with him at Rochford Hall in Essex. She died in 1543.

In 1535 the vivacious and flirtatious Madge (or Margaret) Shelton – known by most of the court as 'the concubine bedded during the pregnancy of the concubine' – appeared on the scene. Extremely pretty and soft-voiced, with dimpled cheeks and a fair complexion, she was originally a lady-in-waiting to her cousin the Queen and governess to Princess Elizabeth. Her father, Sir John Shelton, was commander of the palace guard and cousin to Anne and Mary Boleyn (Sir Thomas Boleyn's sister Anne had married Madge's father), and Henry was attracted to her as he had been to every other member of the Boleyn family.

Madge had so far been unfortunate in her choice of lovers. She had been the mistress of the widowed Sir Henry Norris, Groom of the Stool to Henry VIII, and was betrothed to him in 1536. She had also been the mistress of Sir Francis Weston, initially a page at court and later a gentleman of the household. Both Francis Weston and Henry Norris ended up with their heads on the block on Tower Hill on 17 May 1536, protesting their innocence of the treasonable act of being lovers of Queen Anne.

Madge had been a contributor to the Devonshire Manuscript – a book of two hundred poems written by and circulating within the Boleyn coterie at court – but had been 'wonderfully rebuked' by Anne for defacing a prayer book with 'idle poesies'. Anne required her ladies-in-waiting to carry prayer books at all times, expecting them to spend their time in contemplation of these rather than in idle gossip. Madge never forgot the rebuke and later played a part in the arraignment and trial, conviction and execution of Anne Boleyn and her supposed lovers by quoting, or more likely inventing, remarks she claimed had been made to her by Norris and Weston.

Anne was now becoming more bad-tempered than ever. She knew that Henry had tired of her, but because she also knew that her days were numbered if she failed to bear him a son she ceased to care one way or another about the outcome of the marriage. She would offend him deliberately with her stridently expressed opinions and was often more than mildly contemptuous of his dress and of his views. In or around 1535 Anne decided that Madge should become Henry's mistress. She took the attitude that she would prefer to have a woman in his bed whom she knew, rather than one whom she might not be able to control. Anne knew that Henry was deceiving her with other women and that he had been recently involved with a woman whom she could not identify. She was also unsettled by reports from the French ambassador informing her that Henry had found new lovers. She had failed him by not providing an heir. The end of the road was fast approaching, and she feared that divorce was inevitable. That Henry had lost interest in divorce after the headache involved in obtaining one from Queen Catherine had not occurred to her. If it had done she would certainly have been more diplomatic in her remarks, rather than spitefully doing her best to douse the flames of her husband's grandiosity.

The fifty-year-old Catherine of Aragon died early in 1536. Always a man happy to bury his mistakes, Henry was delighted with the news. Mrs Amadas, the wife of Robert Amadas, keeper of the King's Jewel House was also delighted. Given to tantrums and strange visions, she had previously got into trouble for prophesying that Anne Boleyn would be burned at the stake within six months of her marriage to Henry – a prediction born of jealousy, for she was herself a mistress of the King. Happy to be rid of someone whom she must have thought of as her rival, she made no secret of the fact that she and Henry had, around 1528, often used Sir William Compton's house in Thames Street for their meetings when they were intimate.

By chance, Anne was pregnant once again, and Henry was certain that this time it would be a boy. He was right, but in the excitement of the 'death celebrations' for Catherine – which had as usual included over-eating and 'much merriment' and dancing – Anne miscarried and delivered a stillborn son at the end of January. Knowing that her fate was now sealed, she prophetically declared, 'I have miscarried of my saviour.' She was right. She expected divorce, but she had forgotten her rejection of Henry when he was overwhelmingly in love with her. Never one to forgive a grudge or to forget one, Henry now falsely accused her of infidelity with five men including her brother George. Only one of them 'confessed' to his crimes without recourse to the rack, but that was enough. Infidelity was a treasonable offence in a queen (but clearly not in a king), and the penalty was execution.

The only concession Henry made to his Queen and one-time beloved mistress (reassuring himself that there was much good in him) was to arrange that, instead of being burned alive – the usual penalty for a woman convicted of high treason – Anne would be beheaded with a specially sharpened sword instead of an axe, to be used by a skilled executioner brought from France especially for the occasion. He told her it would be less painful. He ordered her execution to take place not in public but privately, as she had requested, on the green within the Tower on 19 May 1536, four days after her sentence was passed – to allow time for him to divorce her. Anne went peacefully to her death after praying tearfully for God's forgiveness for her sins. The French executioner asked her also to forgive him for carrying out his orders. She did so and paid him his fee. She had tied her long hair into a knot on top of her head, and, having removed her necklace, she was decapitated skilfully and swiftly – just as her husband had promised. As the headsman held her head high and shouted 'So perish all the King's enemies!' the onlookers were horrified to see Anne's lips moving and her eyes turning to one side. She was dead but not brain dead until these last terrifying moments had passed.

No concessions were made to the five men accused of being her lovers other than having their sentences commuted from being hanged, drawn and quartered to being beheaded with an axe. Catholics – who saw Anne as the cause of the King's break with Rome – were overjoyed by Anne's death, but their happiness was short-lived, since Henry made it clear that he had no intention of revoking his decision to appoint himself Supreme Head of the Church.

The overt aim of Henry's multiple liaisons was to procreate. When he did so successfully, he believed that his powers of leadership had been enhanced. He deluded himself into believing that, by impregnating women, he empowered both them and himself. If the women failed to conceive or lost interest in him, he behaved as if they had robbed him of his potency and had in effect castrated him. When he allowed himself to be persuaded that Anne Boleyn had committed adultery, despite the absence of any evidence, he retaliated in kind by metaphorically castrating her in turn: he had her beheaded. Her crowning glory, the symbol of female power, was no more. Anne's treasonable offence was not just her failure to demonstrate her husband's virility and therefore his power: she had also supposedly shared the secrets of the bedchamber with another. Decapitation was the ultimate punishment. It was not difficult for Henry to convince himself that the woman who had stolen his potency by giving it to another man was offering his rival 'his head on a plate'. The logical penalty for attempting the treasonable offence of dislodging the crown was to behead the offender.

Henry succumbed to ostentatious displays of joy on the deaths of both Catherine of Aragon and Anne Boleyn. He dressed in fine yellow clothing (the colour of royal mourning in Spain at the time) and stuck a feather in his cap when Catherine died and could barely contain himself while waiting for the sound of the cannon announcing that Anne Boleyn was no more. When he heard it, he immediately announced his betrothal to Jane Seymour. Archbishop Cranmer had given him dispensation to do so, despite their being distantly related, both being descendants of Edward III.

Henry had been drawn to Jane after his feelings for Anne had turned to resentment. Like almost every other woman he had known, she had been a lady-in-waiting – first to Queen Catherine then, after the divorce, to Queen

Anne. She was easy-going and modest, 'a woman of the utmost charm' but no great beauty, having a wide, angular face, compressed lips, small eyes and a large nose. She was the antithesis of the spirited, lively, flirtatious Madge, in whom Henry now lost interest.

Henry recalled that Anne had invited his suspicion from the very beginning by being more French than English. She had picked up intellectual habits during her youth, which had been spent mostly in France. She also spoke French fluently. He had no difficulty in convincing himself that he had done the right thing by ordering her execution. Jane Seymour was English and thought that Anne deserved her fate.

Within two weeks of Anne Boleyn's death Henry VIII married for the third time. Jane Seymour never argued with her master, and in October 1537, seventeen months after their marriage, she produced a son – Edward. But it was a difficult birth, and after prolonged labour the child was delivered by Caesarean section. In the absence of even minimal antenatal care and more than three hundred years before Joseph Lister's germ theory convinced surgeons of the importance of hygiene in the delivery room, death from infection in mothers and infants was the rule rather than the exception. Edward – later King Edward VI – survived the trauma of his birth, but his mother did not. Twelve days after he was born she inexplicably died from what was most likely puerperal sepsis. Jane Seymour had been a perfect wife, and Henry mourned her passing.

In 1538 it became imperative for reasons of state that Henry marry again. One potential candidate was Christina, the sixteen-year-old widow of Francesco Sforza, Duke of Milan. She was commended to Henry as looking like Madge, and, after Holbein returned with a portrait he had painted of her Henry became lovesick. The far-sighted Christina declined the match, saying that if only she had been born with *two* heads one of them would certainly have been at His Majesty's disposal.

No other royal woman in Europe was prepared to take the risk of marrying Henry until Anne of Cleves volunteered to do so. But no sooner had they married, in January 1540, than they both realized that they were wrong for each other, and soon afterwards they underwent a mutually agreed annulment. By now Henry's body was no longer what it had been. Anne found him and his ulcerated leg repulsive, but she tried not to agree to the annulment too quickly, for she thought she knew what his reaction would be. Henry was only too pleased to be rid of her, however. He found her unattractive and dull. As a result of her diplomacy, Anne became the first of all his wives with whom he remained on friendly terms. Henry gave her a generous settlement and two grand houses. She was often invited to court, and the King referred to her as his sister.

Within three weeks of the annulment, on 28 July 1540 Henry married wife number five. Catherine Howard was Anne Boleyn's first cousin and the niece of the Duke of Norfolk. She was eighteen years old – six years younger than Henry's daughter Mary – and 'a rose without a thorn' according to the King but naïve and flirtatious according to those who knew her better. She appointed her admirers to her official posts and had affairs with several of them. Unfortunately for Catherine, however, this 'rose' proved to have two thorns – both of them men. The delinquent bride was executed on 13 February 1542 on the same spot as her cousin Anne.

Henry never gave up. By now he was looking for a carer rather than a sexual partner, and Catherine Parr seemed ideal. Though she was in love with Jane Seymour's brother, she knew that she might not have long to wait for him if she first married the King. Though she barely escaped the Tower for contradicting a now dementing Henry – in the throes of (probably syphilitic) mental deterioration – she was right. Henry died less than four years after their marriage, on 28 January 1547, thirty-eight years after he had come to the throne – without a woman to comfort him. Catherine, who had not been summoned to the King's deathbed, was now free to marry the man she loved. But she was soon betrayed. Thomas Seymour was thought to have been unfaithful to her after their marriage with Henry's daughter Elizabeth. Catherine Parr died in her bed in childbirth on 7 September 1548.

After Henry's death many of his 'friends' and one-time mistresses felt free to comment on their relationships with the once powerful king who no longer posed a threat to them. Elizabeth Bryan, married to the diplomat Sir Nicholas Carew, was a striking beauty and the sister of Henry's intimate friend Sir Francis Bryan – a poet, diplomat, debauched companion and notable rake and hell-raiser, who reported how the King, in Calais, once called for 'a soft bed and a hard harlot'. Henry gave Elizabeth 'many diamonds and pearls and striking jewels' that were not his to give but were the property of the Queen. Jane Seymour had stayed at Carew's house while Anne Boleyn was awaiting execution and had been kept informed of all the gruesome details by Sir Francis.

The King's physician, Dr John Chamber, now felt free to describe the King as 'overly fond of women' and 'given to lustful dreams'. And a contemporary biographer of Henry, William Thomas, said that 'it cannot be denied that he was a very fleshly man and no marvel, for albeit his father brought him up in good learning, yet after, he fell into all riot and overmuch love of women'. A later Catholic observer claimed reasonably accurately that 'King Henry gave his mind to three notorious vices: lechery, covetousness and cruelty but the latter two issued and sprang out of the former.'

During the lifetime of the King, to speak against him invited the death sentence. Many died needlessly and cruelly for an offence that took centuries to evolve into freedom of speech. Hundreds were hanged, revived with vinegar, then disembowelled and quartered, and others who dared to speak openly of the tyranny of Henry's reign were disembowelled, quartered and *then* hanged. Henry practised religious discrimination, stole the assets of the Catholics and killed those who protested. He destroyed monasteries and he burned books. It was not enough for him to have his fifth wife, the twenty-year-old Catherine Howard, beheaded: he also had her lover, Thomas Culpepper, tortured to death. Henry's legacy was state-sponsored terrorism, discrimination based on religion, contempt for women and the moral and financial bankruptcy of his subjects.

—2—

Charles II

And So to Bed

Lucy Walter, Barbara Villiers, Louise de Kéroualle, Hortense de Mazarin and Nell Gwyn were among the women who featured in the life of Charles II – England's 'merry monarch' – as were Winifred Wells, Mrs Jane Roberts, Mrs Knight, Mary (the widowed Countess of Falmouth) and Elizabeth, Countess of Kildare. Some were commoners and some were courtiers. Some of these were single, some were married. Some had children, and one or two were lesbians. They had little in common with one another, and all that Charles asked was that they be sexually accomplished and verbally flattering.

Charles II, second son of Charles I, was born on 29 May 1630 at St James's Palace. His older brother, also Charles, had died a year earlier at Greenwich Palace a few hours after his birth. His mother had gone into premature labour, owing, it was thought, to her having been jumped on the previous day by her pet mastiff.

King Charles I was on his way to St Paul's Cathedral to give thanks for the birth of a healthy second son when he was relieved to see a more than usually bright morning star. In seventeenth-century England this was considered a happy portent. The King was even more overjoyed when two days later this was followed by an almost total eclipse of the sun. If these were in fact portents, they turned out to be unhappy ones.

While the future King Charles II's parents were attractive in appearance, their baby was not. Charles's mother, Queen Henrietta Maria, daughter of King Henri IV of France, wrote to her former nanny that the child was so ugly she was ashamed of him. But she added that his size and features supplied the want of beauty. He was dark, fat and swarthy, and on reaching adulthood he immediately began to look for women who admired his looks and who professed to negate his mother's view of him. Yet he was never completely reassured. When, aged forty, he saw Sir Peter Lely's portrait of him he exclaimed, 'Odd's fish, I am an ugly fellow!'

From the time of his birth Charles was both a disappointment and a joy not only to his mother and father, whose expectations he often failed to live up to, but also to his country, which was divided not only by religion but by uncertainty over the relative merits of monarchy and republic. Charles grew up trying to steer a middle course when at the time no middle course existed. At the beginning of the first civil war between the parliamentarians and the royalists, the twelve-year-old Charles and his younger brother James were at their father's side at the Battle of Edgehill in October 1642. Despite the obvious danger Charles I had put his sons in, he was determined that they would survive the war and ensure his inheritance. He entrusted Charles to their mother, who in 1646 eventually took him to France. James, his younger son, had been captured at Oxford in that same year and was imprisoned in St James's Palace until two years later, disguised as a girl, he was helped to escape.

Charles loved his mother, though she kept him on a tight reign. During the eleven years of his exile he was both emotionally and financially dependent upon her. The King of France had offered to help them, but his mother did not think it fitting for the heir to the English throne to depend upon anyone but herself. Charles resented the meagre allowance that his mother gave him, and ultimately her meagre interest in him. When he was old enough he transferred himself to Holland, leaving his mother in France.

Charles had been born into political insecurity and war. He grew up with an embattled father and an exhausted mother. Henrietta Maria, who was fifteen when she married the King, was pregnant with one or other of her four sons and five daughters for much of Charles's childhood. Throughout his early years his constant companion was a wooden baton that he carried with him everywhere. At a time when the future was uncertain, the superstitious looked for signs that the gods were with them and the baton came in for comment. Charles's friends presciently said that he would rule with a club rather than with a sword, but his enemies likened his baton to the log of

Aesop's fable in which the frogs, saddened by the absence of a strong ruler, ask Jupiter to send them a king. A huge log is cast down into the lake. The enormous splash causes the frogs to flee in terror to the bottom of the pool. But it was not long before they recognize the inert and motionless log for what it is and ask Jupiter to send them another sovereign. No one saw the baton as a child's transitional object to which Charles could turn for comfort when his parents were unavailable. The fact that it was a club rather than a cuddly toy might suggest that it was perhaps his father whom he missed more than his mother.

As a child King Charles I had been frail and delicate. He had suffered from a severe stammer and rickets and was unable to walk or talk until he was almost four years old. At times it was thought that he would not survive into adulthood. In 1603 he was too ill to travel from Scotland to London for the accession of his father James I to the throne and was left behind in the care of servants. As a young child the only constant in his life was his older brother Henry, who died in November 1612, when Charles was not quite twelve years old. He was tutored by a Scottish Presbyterian and was regarded as an intellectual with, at first, little or no interest in the political life of his country. In addition to the loss of his older brother, his much loved sister Elizabeth left England a year later to live with her husband, Frederic, Elector Palatine and later King of Bohemia, in Germany. In 1619, six years after this second loss, he was in mourning for his mother, Queen Anne. Growing to be only five feet four inches tall, Charles appears in his portraits, most of them painted by Sir Anthony Van Dyck, as long-faced and depressed.

Only three months after his son's wedding in 1625, James I of England died from porphyria – a disease later to become known as 'the royal malady' – and Charles found himself king of a country divided. His marriage at the age of twenty-four to Princess Henrietta Maria was not universally welcomed in England, because of his wife's Catholic faith. Though he did not find his new wife attractive, he hoped that in the course of time he would reconcile himself both to her looks and to her lack of scintillating conversation.

Parliament distrusted him. A Catholic sympathizer in a country more attracted to Puritanism, Charles I found himself involved in two civil wars between royalists and parliamentarians. He lost both. While in the second war he had the support of the Scots, who felt obliged to come to the rescue of a Stuart king, this did not help him. In 1649 the future Charles II was devastated when his father was tried at Westminster Hall and later beheaded at the Palace of Whitehall in London. Begging Cromwell to spare his father's life, Charles had sent Cromwell a signed sheet of blank paper on which he invited him to list whatever he desired, undertaking to deliver anything that was asked for. Cromwell was not interested: Charles I had been put on trial for waging war against his people, had been found guilty and was to pay the penalty.

During his eleven years in exile, the future Charles II saw it as his duty to recover the lost thrones of Scotland and England. It was not until 1660, two years after the death of Oliver Cromwell, that the army, under the command of the royalist General Monck, invited him to return and be proclaimed King Charles II. The Catholic world of his mother rejoiced, though the Puritans were understandably disappointed, fearing that Charles would be influenced by his mother's faith and by her French birth.

Charles sailed from Holland to Dover and then, with his household, returned to London, arriving on 29 May 1660, his thirtieth birthday. He was overjoyed, and so were his people. The eleven dull republican years, lightened momentarily for him by comfort in sexual excesses, had come to an end, and the new King looked forward if not to peace then at least to prosperity in the land of his birth. Charles's popularity decreased when it was eventually realized how much the country was in debt to France. But the country forgave him even when, in 1672, Dutch warships sailed up the Medway and towed the *Royal Charles* back to Holland after sinking most of the British fleet. Determined that austere republicanism should be put behind them, the British people continued to celebrate the restoration of the monarchy.

While an exile from his motherland, uncertain of his status and without a father on whom to model himself, Charles had been unhappy with his appearance. He had a thin face, framed by a mass of black curls, and during his years in France and Holland he had looked to women to reassure him that he was not an unattractive loser but someone to be admired.

Despite the several mistresses he had while in exile, it was only when he returned to England that he had the courage to acknowledge himself not as an abandoned prince but as a king and, more importantly, one whose status he intended to confirm by making a noble marriage. When the time came, Charles, like his ancestor Henry VIII, sought out a wife who was politically suitable and had an attractive dowry, and who, it was hoped, would be capable of providing him with an heir. While in the sixteenth century Henry VII had looked to Spain for a bride for his son and for an ally for England, Charles in the seventeenth century looked to Portugal.

Though she had never seen him, Princess Catherine, the 22-year-old daughter of King John IV of Portugal, had fantasized about being in love with Charles since her childhood. As the Infanta Princess Catherine of Braganza, she had been unofficially betrothed to Charles, then fourteen, since she was seven and had grown up with a romantic image of the future King of England which never left her. Charles's mother, Queen Henrietta Maria, had met Catherine and reassured her son that he would find her adorable, but Charles had already decided that he loved her from her portrait. Though he was unattracted by what he considered to be her bizarre hairstyle (her curls were arranged in two stiff pyramids from which her hair hung in corkscrews), he found her eyes expressive and full of beauty. He knew little else about his future wife, who for five years had been kept a virtual prisoner in the royal palace (presumably to protect her from unsuitable suitors). She had been bred, as it was said at the time, 'hugely retired'.

Being looked at, and admired for his appearance, was almost more important to him than his bride's attractiveness. He did not doubt his virility, which had been successfully tested many times over before he met her, but he had serious doubts as to whether he was himself lovable.

Catherine was familiar with the gossip about Charles. Her ladies-in-waiting had told stories of his many mistresses, but she was not put off by them. Had she known that his sexual needs were virtually insatiable she might have thought twice about what she was letting herself in for. The little she did know made her more attracted to him. If so many women loved him, she told herself, it would be a privilege to be among them. If it turned out, as she fervently hoped, that Charles came to love her, then she would be displacing them. Having heard of the signed letter Charles had sent to

Cromwell pleading for his father's life, Catherine was filled with admiration for the efforts he had made to prevent his father's execution. She saw her future husband as a family man whom she could love, and she decided that, though she was a devout Catholic, she would embrace not only her betrothed but also his religion. Her illusions about the holiness of the state of matrimony into which she had entered were soon dashed.

For the moment, however, she was in no doubt about her destiny and was looking forward to her new status. Charles sent his fleet to bring her from Lisbon to England. Fourteen warships left on the morning of 25 April 1662 and, with a retinue of over a hundred courtiers and servants, a dowry of £360,000 and written undertakings that the Portuguese naval bases of Bombay and Tangier would be transferred to England, Catherine was transported to her beloved in the *Royal Charles*, the flagship of the English battle fleet. A month later, on 21 May 1662, she married the man of her dreams in a private Catholic ceremony at Portsmouth, her port of disembarkation. This was followed in the evening by a Protestant ceremony conducted by the Bishop of London. That day the King wrote to the Lord Chancellor, Edward Hyde, 1st Earl of Clarendon:

If I have any skill in physiognomy, which I think I have, she must be as good a woman as ever was born. Her conversation as much as I can perceive, is very good, for she has wit enough, and a most agreeable voice. You would wonder to see how well acquainted we are already. In a word, I think myself very happy, for I am confident that our two humours will agree very well together.

The bride and her groom spent a few days in Portsmouth, presumably consummating their marriage, before travelling to London.

What Catherine did not know until her arrival was that after his return from exile Charles had arranged for his current mistress to join him. Barbara Palmer, née Villiers, his lover for some two years, had done her best to poison the King's mind against Catherine and to delay the King's journey from London to Portsmouth to welcome her. Heavily pregnant with his child, she threatened to kill herself if he left her. On Charles's return with his bride,

Barbara – who was renowned for both her beauty and her sexual promiscuity – arranged for her underwear to be hung to dry in the palace grounds in full view of the royal bedroom.

Barbara was born in 1641 in the ward of St Margaret's Westminster. Her father was William Villiers, Viscount Grandison, a royalist nobleman who fought at Edgehill alongside Charles's father. In 1643 he died of his war wounds. Barbara's mother, Mary Bayning, daughter of Viscount Bayning, remarried soon after – to Charles Villiers, Earl of Anglesey, a relatively impoverished member of her late husband's family – and took little interest in caring for her daughter.

Totally dissatisfied with her home life, Barbara began her sexual adventures when she was fifteen. When she finally made her appearance in London, in 1656, she was 'dressed in a very plain country dress', being too poor to wear anything more fashionable. Long before she was introduced to Charles she had had several lovers, Philip Stanhope, the second Earl of Chesterfield, being one of the earliest. She became his mistress when she was sixteen and he was twenty-three, a father and already a widower. With Barbara making most of the running, the intermittent relationship lasted until 1660. Then she caught smallpox and Chesterfield lost interest – though her beauty was unaffected – and he was also obliged to escape to France after killing an opponent in a duel.

Barbara first met Prince Charles when she and her husband, the cavalier Roger Palmer, travelled to Holland to offer their financial support for his campaign to recover his throne. Charles not only accepted Palmer's offer of £1,000, which was intended as a quid pro quo for preferment, but also took his wife – though Palmer knew nothing of this at the time. Charles wrote to thank him for the money: 'You have more title than one to my kindness,' he told him – perhaps hoping that this turn of phrase might one day be useful in defending himself against a charge of stealing his wife, by indicating Palmer's complicity.

Barbara had married Roger Palmer, a student at the Temple, a year earlier, on 14 April 1659, after her lover Lord Chesterfield had shown no sign that his intentions towards her were honourable. Palmer's father, a well-to-do country knight, was so alarmed at Barbara's already black reputation that he warned his son that if he were to persist in marrying her he would live to be the most miserable man in the world. The prediction proved correct. Barbara had her first child, Anne, in 1661. The father could well have been Roger Palmer or Charles II or even possibly Lord Chesterfield.

It was not until October 1661 that Charles recognized his mistress officially, by granting the angry Palmer an Irish earldom, its inheritance being limited to 'heirs of his body gotten on Barbara Palmer his now wife'. As the wife of Lord Castlemaine, Barbara was able to enjoy the privileges of rank. Palmer had wanted preferment and had been willing to pay for it but had not thought the price would include his wife. Mortified by her duplicity, he never took his seat in the Irish House of Lords and rarely used his title. The more immediate reason for his ennoblement, however, was that Barbara was expecting Charles's child and insisted on this. A boy was born on 18 June 1662 and christened Charles Fitzroy, though it was thirteen years before Charles acknowledged the boy as his.

Barbara had wanted to give birth at Hampton Court, but even Charles thought this indelicate and a slur on his new bride. Some would say that even more indelicately, but certainly conveniently, he agreed to place his mistress's name at the top of the list of appointees as ladies of the bedchamber to his new Queen. Catherine, whose loving feelings for Charles had not changed when she finally met him, was so shocked when she was unexpectedly introduced to Barbara Villiers – whose reputation had preceded her – that her nose began to bleed profusely and she had to be carried from the room. When she had recovered her composure she argued against having her husband's mistress as one of her ladies-in-waiting, but, with as yet no allies outside her native Portugal, she was obliged to accept Barbara's appointment and the humiliation that accompanied it.

Barbara's sway over Charles was virtually complete. Prisoner of his libido, he was for most of the time out of touch with his intellect. The baptism of Barbara's child provoked dissension between the Palmers, since Barbara had the child baptized for a second time, with the King as witness, after he had already received a Catholic baptism authorized by Roger

Palmer. Barbara, who had sworn that the baby had received no previous blessing, was enraged by her husband's 'disloyalty' in implying that she had lied and stripped bare the marital home in King Street before abandoning it. Roger left for France immediately, and as soon as he was out of her way she returned triumphantly to the house.

According to his diaries, Samuel Pepys spent his nights dreaming of Barbara Villiers. In 1665 – having dreamed that he had her in his arms and 'was admitted to use all the dalliance [he] desired with her' – he wrote 'what a happy thing it would be, if when we are in our graves . . . we could dream . . . such dreams as this – that then we should not need to be so fearful of death as we are at this plague-time'. Sir Peter Lely, who painted her a number of times – including with her head resting on the back of her hand, looking like a penitent virgin, which she undoubtedly was not – declared that 'It is beyond the compass of art to give this lady her due as to her sweetness and exquisite beauty.' Pepys, still carried away by his sexual fantasies, described her as 'a little lecherous girl when she was young and used to rub her thing with her fingers or against the end of forms . . . I know well enough she is a whore.' He implied that Barbara's celebrated sexual athleticism resulted from her studying the salacious works of the sixteenth-century Italian poet Pietro Aretino. Pepys was wrong: Barbara Villiers's compulsive sexual need to convert all her lovers into fathers was one probably driven by the loss of her own father when she was less than two years old. Envying Charles his good fortune in having her as his mistress, Pepys considered whether the King would welcome his guidance on the affair, but concluded in the words of an Italian proverb that 'a man with an erection is in no need of advice.'

Barbara was infamous throughout the kingdom, and a poem based on the rumour that she had forced her attentions on one of her coachmen went as follows:

> She through her lackey's drawers as he ran,
> Discern's love's cause and a new flame began
> Full forty men a day have swiv'd the whore
> Yet like a bitch she wags her tail for more

John Wilmot, Earl of Rochester, wrote his poem 'The Mistress' with Barbara and Charles in mind:

> Nor are his high Desires above his strength
> His sceptre and his —— are of a length
> And she that plays with one may sway the other
> And make him little wiser than his brother.

He commented that 'an age in her embraces past, / Would seem a winter's day'. But referring to the King as 'A merry monarch, scandalous and poor' resulted in his being banned from the court.

Other men with whom Barbara had affairs included Sir Charles Berkeley (who acted as a go-between for Charles and Barbara), James Hamilton (Charles's Groom of the Bedchamber), Lord Sandwich and Henry Jermyn, as well as James Scott (also known as James Fitzroy and James Crofts, Charles's son, born in 1649, by his earlier mistress Lucy Walter). But her conquests were not all courtiers, though these were conveniently to hand. On one occasion she surprised herself by forming a liaison with a rope-dancer. She should perhaps not have been surprised: her life had been one long balancing act not only between lovers but between approval and disapproval.

By the time that Charles entered London in procession with his new bride, Barbara had created so much controversy at court that Clarendon, the Lord Chancellor, though a close friend of her father's, was unable to bring himself to mention her by name. The Dowager Duchess of Richmond reminded her of the fate of Jane Shore, the mistress of King Edward IV, who had died in poverty and whose body was flung on a dunghill. A few days later three masked men accosted Barbara in St James's Park and verbally abused her. They, too, reminded her of the fate of Jane Shore. Though the King's guard searched the park as quickly as possible, the culprits were never found. There seemed to have been a concerted effort by Charles's court to frighten his mistress away, but little came of it other than her resolve that one day she would rid the King of his Lord Chancellor. With Charles's protection, she withstood all the attacks made against her.

In 1663 the arrival from France of Frances Stewart, who was sent by

Charles's sister, Henriette-Anne ('Minette'), Duchesse d'Orléans, to be Catherine's maid of honour, coincided with a serious illness suffered by Catherine. Frances – granddaughter of Lord Blantyre – was said to be one of the most beautiful women of her day and was the model for the image of Britannia stamped on British coins. The antithesis to Barbara Villiers, she was pretty rather than voluptuous, artless rather than witty, virtuous rather than available and childishly yet stupidly vain. Charles was besotted with her – though his feelings were not reciprocated. On one occasion, unable to cope with rejection, he cancelled his appointments for the afternoon, found a small rowing boat and rowed himself down the Thames to Somerset House, where Frances was living. Finding the gates locked, he clambered over the wall in order to see her. She was one of the few women who was wooed by the King but declined to become his mistress. In April 1667, when she could no longer avoid his attentions without incurring his great displeasure, she eloped with her cousin the Duke of Richmond.

Barbara's influence temporarily waned while Charles spent his time trying to overcome Frances's reluctance to have sex with him. Her sexual power over him was such, however, that she soon bounced back. And, not satisfied with the success of her seductive charms, she sought additional status by meddling in politics. By 1663 she not only had a room next to the King's own quarters but had also supplanted Charles's chosen advisers with men of her own recommendation. She undermined the efforts of Louis XIV's ambassadors to bring about peace between England and Holland. As the British fleet burned at Chatham in the Medway, following a daring raid by the Dutch in 1667, Barbara distracted the King to such an extent that he spent the evening chasing moths with her at his daughter-in-law's house. The peace treaty signed at Breda later that year provided her with the chance to help get rid of the increasingly unpopular Lord Chancellor, the censorious Lord Clarendon, who liked the Queen but certainly did not like Barbara.

In 1663 Barbara had again become pregnant by Charles. When he denied paternity she was furious with him, but he later gave her expensive presents – probably not so much because he loved her but because of a belated sense of guilt. In 1665, when she was once more pregnant, Barbara threatened to kill the child if he again denied paternity. Charles had no wish to cope with her histrionics. He no longer needed to worry about adverse comment, since everyone – including his wife – knew about his affair. Despite his mistress's threats, he knew he must give her up, though this was inevitably a gradual process and took about twelve years to complete. Barbara had already provided the King with four bastard children – Anne, Charles, Henry and Charlotte Fitzroy – and in 1666 her latest pregnancy resulted in another son, George. But now, almost as a self-fulfilling prophecy, she had contrived to lose her lover as she had lost her own father.

In fact she used one man after another to satisfy her addictive needs and never gave up the search for a father figure. If she was unable to find one, she created one by becoming pregnant. One lover after another came and went. When she thought that she had found her lost father in another man, her interest in sexual activity with him often ceased after the birth of her child – probably because of the incest barrier. Charles did not come into this category, however, possibly because she never loved him in the first place. Her relationship with him empowered her to such an extent that all other considerations were swept aside

John Churchill, son of the first Sir Winston and later the first Duke of Marlborough, was another lover whom Barbara lost no time in turning into a father. In July 1672, when she was thirty-one and he twenty-two, she had a daughter by him. In 1675 yet another lover, the dramatist William Wycherley, seemed to have based much of the sexual innuendo and *double entendre* in *The Country Wife* – then being performed in London – with his mistress in mind. Barbara, who did not expect any man to value her, would hardly have been surprised, had she been aware of the connection, when Wycherley's Harcourt says, 'Mistresses are like books. If you pore upon them too much, they doze you and make you unfit for company; but if used discreetly you are the fitter for conversation by 'em.' Another character, Dorilant, comments, 'A mistress should be like a little country retreat near the town, not to dwell in constantly, but only for a night and away, to taste the town better when the man returns.'

There were other affairs Barbara preferred to forget. These included a relationship with the dandy Beau Feilding – nicknamed 'Handsome' Feilding by Charles II – and one with the highwayman and 'actor' Cardonell

Goodman (known as 'Scum'), who tried to poison two of her sons and ended his days in chains in the Bastille.

Emboldened by Charles's continuing interest in her, in 1667 Barbara demanded that he give orders to release her cousin George Villiers, the Duke of Buckingham, from the Tower of London. He had been imprisoned there for his sleazy attacks upon the King's conduct (which perhaps served as a distraction from the attacks on his own – he had previously been the favourite lover of the homosexual James I). After a furious argument with Barbara Charles set Buckingham free.

This led to a further demand that Charles acknowledge as his the bastard that Barbara was bearing by her lover Henry Jermyn, whose affair with Lady Falmouth drove her into a frenzy of rage. Charles protested that her child could not be his. Pepys noted in his letters that 'for a good while the King's greatest pleasure had been with his fingers, being able to do no more'. Barbara threatened to publish Charles's letters to her, and the King eventually agreed that the child was in fact his.

Tired of his mistress's temper and her insatiable needs, Charles now began to look for a way of ridding himself of her. A plan for her to live in France was rejected because her financial demands were too high. He tried to distance himself by seeking other lovers. Among them was Mary Davis, a dancer described by Pepys as a 'an impertinent slut', and Nell Gwyn, whom Pepys seemed to approve of, referring to her in his diary entry of 3 April 1665 as 'pretty witty Nell'. Charles had promoted Barbara to a position in which she was able to delude herself that she was his social equal. He felt far more comfortable with women who depended on him.

When Charles's second natural son, Henry, was acknowledged by him and married to the daughter of the Earl of Arlington, one of Barbara's old friends, he loaded honours on the boy. In the previous year Barbara had 'kidnapped' Mary Wood, the daughter of the wealthy Sir Henry Wood, Clerk of the Green Cloth – another lover – to ensure a satisfactory marriage for her eldest son, Charles Fitzroy. True to her reputation for greed and rapacity (she was accustomed to losing £20,000 at the card game of basset and wearing jewellery worth £40,000 in the currency of the time), Barbara set about extracting further titles and pensions for herself.

Charles eventually wrote to her, 'Madam, all that I ask of you for your own sake is, live so for the future as to make the least noise you can, and I care not who you love.'

In 1677, after Charles had given her up, Barbara left England for Paris, where she continued her promiscuous lifestyle and bore two or three more children. This brought the number up to possibly seven or eight from about six different men. Her final 'state' victory was in disposing of the career of her lover the English ambassador Ralph Montagu after a tiff which led to him becoming sexually involved with her daughter Anne. She died on 9 October 1709, at the age of fifty-nine, in Walpole House in Chiswick Mall, the home of her grandson. After a lifetime spent in a search for her lost childhood, she is said to have haunted the house in which she lived, and there are some who believe her restless spirit continues to inhabit it.

Though Barbara Villiers was perhaps the most important, and certainly the most persistent and influential, of the mistresses of Charles II, as we have seen, she was by no means the first. While Charles, barely sixteen, was in Jersey, before going to France and then Holland, his final place of exile, he fathered a child by Marguerite de Carteret, daughter of the governor of the island. The child of this his first recorded liaison was Don Giacomo (James) Stuart, later known as James de la Cloche du Bourg de Jarsey. After he was restored to the throne, Charles supported this son financially and gave him a signed, sealed document for use after his own death to inform Parliament, and his son, of the boy's parentage. The news of his son's birth was kept secret for twenty years, until Charles informed the General of the Jesuits at Rome, asking forgiveness both for him and for 'a young lady who was among the most distinguished in our Kingdom'. The boy was born, he said, 'more from the frailty of our first youth than from any ill intentions or great depravity'.

Charles's next illegitimate child, born in 1651, was a daughter who could have been in no doubt about her parentage. She was given the royal surname Fitzroy and was christened Charlotte Jemima Henrietta Maria. Her mother, eight years older than the twenty-year-old Charles, was the noted beauty Elizabeth Killigrew, the wife of Francis Boyle, later Viscount Shannon. Charlotte herself married James Howard, grandson of the 2nd Earl of Suffolk.

Now living in Bruges, King Charles met Catherine Pegge, daughter of

Thomas Pegge of Yeldesley, Derbyshire. Catherine bore Charles a son, Charles Fitzcharles, and a daughter, Catherine Fitzcharles. In an effort to assuage her guilt, his daughter became a nun and spent her life married to Jesus as Sister Cecilia in Dunkirk, while his son was created Earl of Plymouth and married Lady Bridget Osborne, daughter of the 1st Duke of Leeds. After the Restoration, Charles rewarded Thomas Pegge for the 'loan' of his daughter by creating him a baronet.

Charles's most rapacious concubine during his exile – though not as greedy as some of those with whom he was involved after the Restoration – was Lady Byron, born Eleanor Needham and daughter of Lord Kilmorey. She had been married at the age of eleven to Peter Warburton. Soon widowed, her second marriage was to Lord Byron of Newstead Abbey, Nottinghamshire. Pepys called her 'the King's seventeenth whore abroad', though he was probably quoting court gossip rather than reporting on an audited list. Lady Byron extracted £15,000 from Charles during one of the exile years and later squeezed an annual pension of £500 from him. She enjoyed her pension for only four years, however, dying in 1664.

Unlike the others who – except for Barbara Villiers – had their fifteen minutes of fame and then left, Lucy Walter stayed the course for three years. Between 1648 and 1651 she was Charles's principal mistress. Born in 1630, Lucy was eleven years older than Barbara and, like her, knew Charles in Holland. Pepys, as ever, had something derogatory to say about her: 'It is well known she was a common whore when the King lay with her,' he declared and called her 'a strumpet with not much wit, little means, and less grace'. John Evelyn described her as 'Brown, beautiful, bold but insipid' and noted that, having reached the top as a prostitute during her short life, she died in 1658 of 'a disease incident to her profession'. This was almost certainly syphilis.

Lucy Walter was born at Roche Castle, Pembrokeshire, which was burnt down by Cromwell's men in 1644. When she was eight the family moved to King Street in Covent Garden. Her father was William Walter, squire of the County of Pembroke and previously Comptroller of the Household to Charles I. Her mother, Elizabeth Protheroe, was the niece of the 1st Earl of Carbery. And Lucy had two brothers, Richard and Justus.

Lucy's noble past did little for her future. Her parent's marriage – which had never been a happy one – was marred by violent rows, and by the time Lucy was eleven it had broken down completely. In 1641 her abandoned mother presented a petition to the House of Lords to ask that her husband support her. William counter-petitioned on the grounds that he was owed a dowry of £600, that his wife was 'disloyal and malignant' and that he had 'more than a suspicion of her incontinency'.

Despite being ordered by the House of Lords to return to his wife, Lucy's father refused to do so and his estates were sequestrated. He was nevertheless required to find £60 a year to support her. William left London to live in a house he owned in Wales, while Elizabeth stayed with her sister, who was married to a Dutch merchant. The children were supported by Nicholas Chappell, William's stepfather.

Five years later Elizabeth returned to the House of Lords to recover the arrears of maintenance that her husband had refused to pay on the grounds of her persistent adultery. She claimed that

> She hath so much experience of her husband's disloyalty to her bed and that it is already publicly known that for the space of five years her said husband kept a maid-servant in his house by whom he had two illegitimate children ... and enforced your petitioner to provide for the said children as for his own children lawfully begotten and if at any time she refused to do it (as having just cause) her said husband would revile her beat and abuse her for it.

Lucy's father was awarded custody of his three children, but Lucy had had enough of both her parents and, rather than live with him, she ran away to her uncle's house in The Hague.

Lucy had no reason to like her father, who had always been unkind to her mother and had had little or no time for his children. He not only had not loved her unconditionally but, worse, had probably not loved her at all. On the rare occasions when she saw him, he had abused his role by demanding that she please him by complying with his wishes. Only if she did so would she receive the approval she craved. He may also have insisted that she please him sexually. This seems highly likely because, as an adult, Lucy was able to give her love to a man only if she was being exploited by him. This was true of all her relationships, including that with Charles. However, she treated men with contempt – not hard for a prostitute. Men owed her. She would give none of them what they wanted unless they paid for it in advance. As a child, she had had to pay for love by pleasing her father, and she had no intention of dispensing her own love freely. Her hostility to men was barely below the surface. It is not surprising that in *The Mistresses of Charles II* Brian Masters describes her as 'predatory, given to sulking, and when provoked, liable to react in a demonstrative, ostentatious manner'.

While in Holland, Lucy called herself Mrs Barlow. Having come from a broken home and disowning the parents who had virtually abandoned her, she reinvented herself by taking the name of her mother's brother, John Barlow. At the time she first met Charles, when he was barely sixteen, she was the mistress of Robert Sidney, one of the sons of the Earl of Leicester, having been passed on to Robert by his brother Algernon, a colonel in Cromwell's army, when he was called overseas. According to Evelyn, Robert had bought her services 'for fifty broad pieces of silver'.

When she met Charles again in Holland in the summer of 1648 they soon became lovers. Nine months later she had a son, whom they christened James and who, at the age of thirteen, became the Duke of Monmouth. After the death of his father, James sought to dethrone Charles's brother, James II, believing that as Catherine of Braganza had been unable to supply an heir he himself had a legitimate claim to the throne. Various other royal dukes, all bastard sons of Charles II, felt that they had a claim too, but Monmouth insisted that he took precedence over his three other half-brothers because some thought that his mother and the King had married, either in Haverfordwest in Wales in 1646 or 1647 or in Liège in 1649. Many sources support this contention, and the courtesy with which Lucy was treated by members of the King's family also lends support to this belief.

While the King greatly valued his son by Lucy, his mother neglected the boy's well-being and education. She had as little time for him as her parents had had for her. Understandably, given her upbringing, she had plenty of time for herself. Her unsubstantiated claim that she and Charles were man and wife contributed to the tension between Charles and his followers on the one hand and Lucy on the other. Because of her son's potential position in the affairs of state, at least one attempt to kidnap him was made by royalist factions hostile to the King.

Lucy was not altogether loyal to Charles. Lord Taafe, Charles's effective Chamberlain while in exile, fathered a girl with her, and Sir Henry de Vic, Charles's representative in Brussels, having become besotted with Lucy, left his post to ask permission to marry her. Another lover was Thomas Howard, brother of the 3rd Earl of Suffolk, Master of the Horse to Charles's sister Mary, the Princess Royal. It was thought that he had been sent to spy on Lucy by Cromwell in order to discredit the King.

Lucy gradually became more and more despised by Charles and his advisers, and this led to her behaviour becoming more extreme, though this could possibly have been due to brain damage caused by syphilis. She returned to London in 1656 and was arrested under Cromwell's orders, interrogated, then released before returning to Brussels and Paris. Charles supported her financially for the two years of life that were left to her.

Lucy's son James went on to meet a particularly grisly end. After the death of his father he was found guilty of treason when he attempted to overthrow his uncle. On the scaffold he complained to the executioner that the blade was not sharp enough. He was right. Three blows of the axe failed to sever his head, which had eventually to be cut off with a knife by the executioner's assistant, the executioner himself having lost his nerve and thrown down the axe.

After Barbara Villiers, Louise de Kéroualle was Charles II's most important mistress. Born Louise Renée Penancoet de Kéroualle in 1649 at Brest, she died at the unusually old age of eighty-five. Her father was Comte Guillaume Penancoet de Kéroualle, a decent, unimaginative and impoverished chevalier. Her mother was a woman of strong religious convictions and, according to Evelyn, both beautiful and shrewd. Louise had a sister, Henriette, and also a brother, Sebastien, who died of wounds received in battle in 1669. John Evelyn's father-in-law, Sir Richard Browne, the King's resident at the court of France for nineteen years, spent much time in Brest between 1652 and 1654 and got to know the Kéroualle family very well. Brest was also a favourite location for exiled Englishmen during the years of the Common-wealth.

'Wondrous handsome', with fair skin, dark hair hanging in ringlets and dark eyes (which had a slight cast, leading Nell Gwyn to call her 'Squintabella'), Louise was described by Evelyn as having a 'childish simple baby face'. Sir Peter Lely's portrait of her, painted when she was about twenty-four, shows her with a petulant and almost patronizing look. She was soft-voiced, with a tendency to pout and a propensity towards tearful-ness. In fact her demeanour was much conditioned by the French court fashion of the time for contrived feminine behaviour.

Louise de Kéroualle was at first chosen to become the mistress of King Louis XIV. Louis gave her up, however, in order to seal the political bond that Charles's youngest sister, Minette, married to the sinister Duc d'Orléans, Louis XIV's brother, had negotiated through the secret Treaty of Dover in 1670. Minette was Charles's favourite sister and would, and prob-ably did, do everything he asked of her during the ten days of revelry that accompanied the signing of the treaty guaranteeing England's support for the French against the Dutch. In return Charles was rewarded with a vast subsidy from the grateful Louis. The death of his sister soon afterwards – probably from peritonitis, though it was suggested at the time that her hus-band might have poisoned her – left Charles deeply upset, for they were very close, incestuously so according to gossip. The French hit upon the idea of sending Louise to London as maid of honour to Queen Catherine – osten-sibly to console Charles but also to be at hand in the palace to watch over their treaty and to use whatever influence she had over Charles to ensure that he would not renege on it.

Charles, as expected, became entranced with Louise. However, it soon became clear to everyone except the King – who as ever allowed his libido to rule his head – that his beloved was a political plant. For nearly two years she held out against Charles's advances, despite the urgings of representatives of the French government that she 'lay down for her country'. All the while she played the King like a fish, which increased his ardour rather than dimin-ished it. She eventually landed him in October 1672, while in the middle of a mock-wedding game organized by Lord and Lady Arlington in which

Charles played the rustic groom and Louise the rustic bride. Nine months later Charles Lennox, the future Duke of Richmond, was born, the fourth of the King's offspring to be born that year, though Charles initially refused to acknowledge paternity. King Louis sent Lady Arlington a diamond necklace as a thank you for her part in his 'conquest'.

Louise had apparently harboured thoughts that she might become Queen upon bearing Charles a son, but unfortunately for her she was disliked by almost everyone, though offered due respect in the King's presence. Her two major disadvantages were, first, that she was obviously a French spy under the direction of Louis XIV and, second, that she was feared as a Catholic.

She also reasoned that she would be accorded more respect if she had titles, and so set about collecting both them and preferments assiduously. Within three years of her arrival at court she became Duchess of Portsmouth, Countess of Fareham and Baroness Petersfield (though the warrants were written to exclude her illegitimate son). She had an annual pension of £10,000 settled on her from revenues from lands in Ireland. And she also used her sexual charms to convince Charles to petition Louis XIV to give her a dukedom in France – which was duly done, though not without reluctance on both sides. She eventually persuaded Charles to recognize his own son and, by trickery, managed to have him given preference over the son of Barbara Villiers. In 1673 she received another gift from Charles: a dose of venereal disease.

Louise's apartments in Whitehall were furnished with such splendour that Charles preferred to receive diplomatic visitors there rather than in his own rooms. Her favourite portrait, painted in the style of the times, shows her stroking a King Charles spaniel as she sits decorously for the artist. Her taste for jewellery was well developed, and her ability to get through money at the gaming tables was prodigious. She supported her own expenditures by selling 'licences to supply' to wine merchants and royal pardons to criminals wealthy enough to afford them, employing a servant especially for the task. But she was far from happy, for she had a miserable time competing for her lover's attention with the declining Barbara Villiers and also, and to an increasing extent, with the actress Nell Gwyn, the rage of the London stage.

Eleanor Gwyn was born in 1650, possibly at her friend Hannah Grace's house in Coal Alley Yard, Drury Lane, London, or in Hereford or in Oxford, where her father, Thomas Gwynne, either a fruit-seller or a captain in Cromwell's army, is said to have died in a debtor's jail. Nell was originally employed as a serving girl in a brothel, possibly run by her mother, before becoming an orange-seller outside the King's Theatre, Drury Lane. Her only sister, Rose, married a highwayman. Rose herself was a thief, who escaped from Newgate jail – and also from her background – because of her connections with the Killigrews, the family who owned the patent for the King's Theatre.

Nell's first sexual experience was probably with the actor-manager Charles Hart, a great-nephew of William Shakespeare, which led to her making the transition to the London stage. By 1665 she was a leading actress. Charles Sackville, Lord Buckhurst – a rake and debauchee – 'bought' Nell from Hart for an allowance of £100 a year and a promise that she could live at his house at Epsom. Soon tiring of his debauchery and his need to act out disagreeable sexual fantasies that were regarded as depraved even in the permissive climate of the time, she returned to London. But, after her liaison with Sackville, Hart would have nothing more to do with her.

In general, however, Nell had an irresistible charm. She was tiny, with extremely small feet, chestnut hair and hazel eyes. She had a deceptively frail appearance and attracted sexually exploitative men who, in an effort to salve their consciences, invariably offered to rescue her from a 'life of prostitution'. She had no difficulty in ridding herself of such hypocrites. She was temperamentally robust and quick-witted as a consequence of her initial employment, and in no need of rescue. Pepys fell in love with her after seeing her playing Florimel in John Dryden's *The Maiden Queen* in 1667.

The King, who loved all things beautiful, was a regular visitor to the theatre – having reintroduced it after the repression of the Puritan era – and Nell got to know him well. It was probably at his behest that by 1670 she had moved to Lincoln's Inn Fields, where she gave birth to his son Charles Beauclerk, the future Duke of St Albans.

Nell Gwyn was the antithesis of Louise de Kéroualle. Perhaps Charles loved them both because they were so different. Nell pretended to be nothing other than an amiable, good-natured working-class girl. She was happy to accept that she was a whore, but told everyone that she was proud to be a Protestant one, unlike the Catholic Louise. Nell and Louise knew that they had to compete for the King's affections. Charles played them off, one against the other, amused at their mutual dislike but delighted to have two women fighting over him. Indeed – now probably at the height of his sexual power but apparently not entirely fulfilled by two mistresses – he became involved with a third. Elizabeth Farley, another actress, presumably filled in gaps left by Nell and Louise. Charles's relationship with her was probably entirely commercial and continued intermittently for several years.

In 1671 Nell was again pregnant and had moved to a Crown-lease house at 79 Pall Mall, now the site of the Army and Navy Club, where she lived until her death with her second son, James Beauclerk, who died aged eight in Paris of an infected leg wound. The house, which had a special lowered wall and a raised mound outside it, allowed garden chats with the King, and Nell was eventually granted the freehold. She pointed out that she gave her services to the King free of charge and was entitled to have a similar courtesy extended to her.

The popular image of Nell Gwyn is that, in contrast with her haughtier rivals for Charles's affections, she was known for her kindness and consideration for others. The facts seem to bear this out. Among other things she looked after her ageing mother, who lived with her until the day in 1679 when she fell into a ditch in a drunken stupor and was drowned. Nell is also credited with encouraging Charles to support the Chelsea Hospital for retired servicemen, founded in 1681 and officially opened in 1692.

Nell's final years were spent comfortably, though mostly in debt, until – nearly three years after the death of the King – she died from venereal disease in November 1687. Charles is said to have remembered her with his dying words 'Let not poor Nelly starve', and his successor, James II, was happy to comply with his brother's wish, for he knew that if Charles had had a legitimate heir he himself would not have acceded to the throne. Charles's fourteen illegitimate children were discounted.

In the meantime Louise's star was waning further. She now had to contend with the solar power of Hortense Mancini, Duchesse de Mazarin, an aristocratic beauty who had fled her native France disguised as a man.

According to her many admirers, Hortense Mazarin was the wildest and the most beautiful of all of Charles's mistresses. She was sexually promiscuous, bisexual and a compulsive gambler. Men whose attempts to suppress their own latent homosexuality have not been entirely successful often find gay women attractive. They can allow themselves to be aroused if their homosexual fantasies are being acted out not by men but by women. Whether Charles was a latent homosexual is not known, but it could be argued that he did not much like women – though he desperately wanted them to like him – since he turned his back on one after another in his search for the ultimate in gratification, despite giving each one the impression that she was important to him.

Hortense's sexual preferences represented a challenge which would have appealed to his competitive spirit. Hortense was also intelligent and possessed of an engaging personality in addition to good looks. Charles was unable to resist her attractions. When she arrived in London, in 1675, she was impoverished as a result of her husband's extravagance and totally dependent on any man with money.

The niece of Cardinal Mazarin, sometime Prime Minister of France, she had been married at thirteen to a duke. Her uncle died soon after the marriage and left her a vast fortune, which her greedy and disagreeable husband lost no time in squandering. Hortense's appeal to Louis XIV to help her regain her assets fell upon deaf ears. It had once been suggested that she marry Charles II while he was in exile in France. He was keen, but she was not, and to his dismay she had turned him down. However, on her arrival in England she lost no time in renewing her acquaintanceship with the King. Hortense's hostility to anything from her native land delighted the English court but dismayed Louise, whose days as an advocate of everything French seemed now to be numbered.

Louise engaged the enemy at close quarters and made a friend – perhaps more than a friend, given Hortense's sexual preferences – of the Duchesse, thereby reimposing her authority over Charles. Hortense took a temporary fancy to a guest of Charles's, the Prince of Monaco, and pursued him relentlessly for a brief period, thereby insulting Charles and casting Louise in a more loyal light.

Surviving the anti-Catholic terror aroused by the supposed Popish Plot to depose Charles in 1678, Louise was invited to France, where she dazzled the French court with her wealth and self-assurance. She came back even more bolstered in her own esteem and resumed her quest for wealth and power by taking over the functions of the Queen at dinners and state banquets.

Louise tripped up only when she fell for the odious nephew of Hortense de Mazarin, Philippe de Vendôme, Grand Prior of France. Philippe's outrageous behaviour so incensed Charles that Louise's relationship with the King was again jeopardized. But Charles's own lack of fidelity gave him a forgiving nature where others' trespasses were concerned, and the relationship resumed as strong as ever. Throughout his philanderings, unlike his equally sexually rapacious predecessor Henry VIII, Charles rarely showed jealousy or envy. He was never violent and beheaded none of his rivals on flimsy political excuses. He believed in live and let live.

On 2 February 1685 the 54-year-old Charles was struck down by a stroke, and, after a frantic regime of drugs, purging, bleeding, cauterizing and blistering, within a few days he was dead. Despite his struggles against Catholicism throughout his life, he was received into the Catholic Church on his deathbed but was buried in Westminster Abbey with Anglican rites. His Queen, to whom in his way he had remained loyal, despite her inability to provide him with an heir, returned to Portugal, where she acted as regent to her brother until her own death in 1705.

On Charles's death, Louise de Kéroualle lost all her influence and was subject to the full force of public opprobrium from which Charles had shielded her. She returned to France, where her high-spending habits gradually led her into penury. Charles's dying words about Nell Gwyn are well known. His last words about Louise are often forgotten: 'I have always loved her and I die loving her.'

King Charles II was no less promiscuous than King Henry VIII, but, unlike his ancestor, he was never anything but courteous to the many women who – seldom for unselfish reasons – agreed to share his bed.

Growing up against a background of war and exile, and powerless to prevent the execution of his father, Charles had looked to women to comfort him in this world, as he eventually looked to the Holy Family to comfort him in the next. His legacies were his children – the bedrock of England's aristocracy – his philanthropy and his paintings. One of the country's most cultured kings, he founded the Royal Society and the Royal Hospital in Chelsea, and many of the pictures he acquired are now to be found in the Royal Collection at Buckingham Palace.

3

James II

And That, Said James, Is That

King Charles II had at least seventeen mistresses and fathered fourteen known illegitimate children but was unable to have a child with his wife Catherine of Braganza. His brother James, Duke of York, who succeeded him as James II, had fewer mistresses but had two daughters, Mary and Anne, from the nine pregnancies of his first wife, Anne Hyde, and a son and a daughter by his second wife, the Catholic Mary of Modena, after five earlier children had died in infancy. As King, his professed intention – somewhat bizarrely, given his behaviour before (and after) acceding to the throne – was to raise the moral tone of the court from the low level to which it had sunk under his brother's rule.

James was born on 14 October 1633. Thirteen years later, during the Civil War, he was captured by the parliamentarians after the surrender of Oxford, the city in which he had been brought up. He was imprisoned in St James's Palace in London, but after two years was helped to escape, dressed as a girl. He travelled first to Holland and then to France, where his brother and mother had also fled for their lives. That his country no longer wanted him or his family made a lasting impression on him, and the resulting fear of rejection and need to have women in love with him were lifelong – though these were emotions more appropriate to the thirteen-year-old he had once been.

James II and his brother grew up together in France with an austere and probably depressed mother and no father, but their reactions to their fractured childhood could not have been more different. James was the baby of the family and was for ever in the shadow of his elder brother. They both sought comfort in the arms of women; but whereas the more passive Charles was content with making conquests and seeking admiration James – more immature, petulant and sometimes violent – was more exploitative and pre-occupied with avoiding rejection.

Their adult interaction with their paramours was based on their perceptions of mothering. Charles's women were for the most part attractive, adult and supportive, and he enjoyed their company. As as soon as he lost interest in them he politely remembered to provide for their future. James's women were, by the standards of the times, often plain and unfeminine. His brother claimed that they were given to him by his confessor – the notorious Father Edward Petre – as punishment for his sins. This judgement, however, is a matter of taste rather than of fact, since portraits of some of James's mistresses show them to have been women of more than average good looks to modern eyes. Charles also said that his brother was as stiff as a mule and that he would lose his kingdom by his bigotry and his soul for a lot of trollops. Indeed, his tastes in women were considered mildly peculiar: Philibert, Comte de Grammont, recalled him commenting, 'No woman's leg is worth anything without green stockings.' This minor stocking fetish throws some light on James's detached attitude to women. The fetish, usually an item of semi-transparent underwear, is an alternative sexual object for many men who feel threatened by female genitals and prefer them partially obscured.

James used women merely as sex objects. His immaturity and possibly paedophile tendencies encouraged him to seek out very young women with undeveloped and boyish bodies. In his mid-thirties he almost married the seventeen-year-old Susan, Lady Bellsyse, the widow of Sir Henry Bellsyse, son of a prominent Roman Catholic statesman. When he changed his mind he was obliged to settle £2,000 a year on her from his estates in Ireland. Gilbert Burnet, Bishop of Salisbury, wrote in *A History of Our Times* that she was 'a woman of much life and great vivacity but of a very small proportion of beauty as the Duke was often observed to be led by his amours to objects that had no extraordinary charms'. In 1674 she was created Baroness of Osgoodby in her own right and became a maid of honour to James's second wife, Mary of Modena, the daughter of Alfonso IV of Modena, who wrote intimate letters to her from exile in France.

When James married Mary he was thirty-nine and she only fifteen –

although as an arranged marriage this was hardly his choice. Despite his many affairs, one is left with the impression that James was not really attracted to feminine women. Like his grandfather, James I, he may have been heterosexual for social reasons but homosexual in his gender preferences.

James had at least eleven mistresses. Because of his fervent – though long concealed – belief in Catholic dogma, he would have experienced strong feelings of guilt. Knowing that what he was doing was contrary to the teachings of a church he so ardently supported may well have increased his sexual arousal when he was with the mistress of the moment, but the battering he received from his conscience when the affair was over invariably left him depressed. Despite his belief in the sanctity of marriage, James could not resist seeking high-risk thrills. He was prepared to fight a civil war to defend the teaching of the Catholic Church, but his compulsive urge to gamble with both his marriage and his conscience led him, when it suited him, to confront Catholic doctrine. Knowing that premarital and extramarital sex were grievous sins for which the withholding of the Blessed Sacrament could be invoked as punishment, he was none the less prepared to take that chance because of his incurable addiction to sex.

Charles believed he was never anything but honest in his behaviour towards women, and expected his brother to behave in much the same way. When Edward Hyde's daughter Anne became pregnant by James, Charles insisted that he marry her. But Anne was not particularly attractive, and it was not long before James became serially unfaithful to her.

Before her marriage, Anne had been strongly attracted to the teachings of the Roman Catholic Church. James – at this time still professing to be an Anglican – tried to use this as an excuse to renege on the marriage. However, Charles II – an expert on mistresses – refused to allow his brother to carry out this deceit. James and Anne finally married in 1660. Ten years later she converted to Catholicism, and soon afterwards she encouraged her husband to do likewise.

After Anne's marriage her father was appointed Earl of Clarendon and later become Lord Chancellor. This was by way of an apology from the self-righteous Charles II for the 'injury' that Hyde had suffered through James's affair with his daughter.

Anne's domineering character led Pepys to comment in 1668, 'In all things but in his cod-piece, [James] is led by the nose by his wife.' Indeed, while still Duke of York, and well into his marriage, James – restless, foolish and scarcely occupied by his appointment as Lord High Admiral of England, Ireland and Wales as well as Lord Warden of the Cinque Ports – continued to look to boyish women for consolation. Anne was renowned for her gluttony, and soothed her anguish over her husband's repeated affairs by resorting to comfort eating. She became increasingly unattractive, and in 1668 Lady Chaworth wrote to Lord Roos that the Duchess 'breaks out so ill of her face visibly – and of her leg again as people talk – that she was yesterday blooded and kept her bed'. Since bleeding and cupping was then the only – albeit largely useless – remedy for most ills, it is hardly surprising that in 1671, at the early age of thirty-four, the bulimic Anne effectively ate herself to death, having done her duty to England by giving her ungrateful husband two living heirs.

Some six years before her premature death, the Duchess of York's name had been linked with that of Henry Sidney, the Earl of Romney. In 1665, while she and James were on a tour in the North of England to escape the plague that was ravaging the capital, she met 'the handsomest man in England', whom she pretended to admire in order to make James jealous. She was pleased to hear from her ladies-in-waiting that Sidney had fallen for her. When James learned of it, like other unfaithful hypocrites he was outraged, and Sidney was banished from the court. Anne, who had put up with her husband's infidelities since their marriage, was delighted that James was jealous of what was probably no more than a minor flirtation. But Sidney never forgave James's vicious reaction, and when he entered Parliament in 1679 he was quick to support – unsuccessful – legislation designed to exclude the Duke of York from the succession to the throne on the grounds that he was secretly a Roman Catholic.

As middle age approached, James became disillusioned and depressed. He began to neglect his appearance and was not well regarded by society. There were complaints that he was not 'ascetic' in his attitude to women and that his sexual indulgences were not in keeping with the prevailing mood of the country. By about 1670 marital infidelity had ceased to be taken for granted, and mutual affection and the sharing of common interests were becoming the new values of society. The public had had enough of Charles II's mistresses and sympathized with his faithful Queen. Disgust at James's abuse of women was expressed by such 'experts' in these matters as Pepys and the suddenly respectable rake Philibert, Comte de Grammont. James's self-approval – never high – sank even further. Both he and his brother Charles had been fit young men during their exile, but in their middle years they had exhausted themselves by lifestyles that had eroded their health. Charles II died at the age of fifty-four in 1685, and James, heavily burdened by his conscience and continuing to suffer a depressive reaction to its complaints, was diagnosed by his contemporaries as suffering from 'God's punishment for his sins'.

James's career as a womanizer had began during his eleven years in exile, and it gathered pace on his return from France in 1660. Back in London he found himself captivated by Goditha Price, a maid of honour to the Duchess of York and sister to one of the Queen's maids of honour, Henrietta Maria Price. The liaison was brief and largely opportunistic. Goditha was there, she caught James's eye, and soon afterwards she found herself in his bed. The affair was supposed to be secret but was known to Pepys because of his close relationship with James.

James's relationship with her successor, the former Elizabeth Butler, 'a virtuous lady', the wife of the 2nd Earl of Chesterfield and the daughter of the Earl of Ormonde, was similarly brief. When she responded to James's advances, her husband – who had never cared for his wife until James became attracted to her – ordered her back to their country estates to forestall the possibility of an affair. The affronted Duchess of York complained to the King about the behaviour of his brother, and for good measure also complained to her father, Lord Clarendon.

Goditha Price and Lady Chesterfield were succeeded by a much more serious relationship that was to end in tragic circumstances. In 1666 James fell in love with the eighteen-year-old Margaret Denham (née Brook), who had recently married the 52-year-old royalist poet Sir John Denham, a husband even more jealous than Lord Chesterfield. During the Civil War, Sir John had acted as a messenger between Charles I in England and his wife,

Henrietta Maria, and their children in France. After the Restoration, when Charles II returned to England to claim his throne, the highly regarded Denham was rewarded by being created Surveyor-General of all the King's buildings, with Christopher Wren as his deputy.

Lady Denham had been introduced to the Duke of York by Lord Henry Brouncker, James's Groom of the Bedchamber. Unlike many of James's mistresses, she was a noted beauty, the embodiment of contemporary ideas of female loveliness, and, in pursuit of what she believed to be her rights she insisted that their relationship be properly acknowledged. In June 1666, at the height of the Anglo-Dutch War of 1665–7, Pepys noted her determination that 'she will not be his mistress, as Mrs Price, to go up and down the privy stairs, but will be owned publicly; and so she is'. Three months later he noted, 'I had the hap to see my Lady Denham . . . and the Duke of York, taking her aside and talking to her in the sight of all the world, all alone.' She also asked to be appointed lady of the bedchamber to James's wife. Anne, needless to say, would not hear of it.

When he discovered that, within a year of her marriage, his wife had taken an obvious interest in the Duke of York, which had been just as publicly reciprocated, Sir John Denham became literally mad with jealousy. He suddenly recovered his sanity when, in January 1667, Lady Denham died after a short and undiagnosed illness. It was widely accepted that he had killed his wife by giving her poisoned chocolate to drink, though there was insufficient evidence for him to face a murder trial. However, there were others who were ready to believe that the murderer was the Duchess of York, who had had enough of her husband's philandering.

When Margaret Denham died, James professed himself heartbroken and swore he would never take another mistress. He was unable to carry out his pledge, however, for almost immediately after her death he fell in love with his wife's new lady-in-waiting, the virtuous Frances Jennings, later Duchess of Tyrconnel. And when she did not respond to his attentions and ignored the love-letters he thrust into her muff he soothed the rejection by turning to another of his wife's ladies-in-waiting, Arabella Churchill, whom he found more responsive.

Born in 1648, Lady Arabella Churchill was the elder sister of John

Churchill, the future Duke of Marlborough, and an ancestor of Sir Winston Churchill. Anthony Hamilton, the Comte de Grammont's brother-in-law, described her as 'a tall creature, pale faced and nothing but skin and bone'. After an initial passionate sexual involvement with the androgynous Arabella, James – who had little experience of women who loved him for himself, rather than for preferment – soon tired of her. His earlier feelings, however, suddenly returned when one day while they were out coursing and Arabella fell off her horse. James was struck by the grace of her limbs and figure as, temporarily concussed, she lay on the ground 'with a most woeful disarrangement of her toilet'. He was probably aroused less by the sight of her underwear than by her dependent need for a rescuer. Playing the role expected of him, he felt his self-assurance returning. In the past he might have chosen unattractive women because he felt that they would be less likely to reject him. Now someone needed him, and he felt the better for it.

The relationship flourished, and Arabella bore him four children: James Fitzjames (born in 1670 and later created Duke of Berwick), Henry Fitzjames (born in 1673 and later created the Duke of Albemarle), Henrietta Fitzjames (who married Lord Waldegrave) and Marie Fitzjames (who became a nun). James Fitzjames was born in Moulins, in France, where Arabella thought it wise to retire during the latter stages of her pregnancy. Later, James served the French throne as a soldier of some distinction in the War of the Spanish Succession and became a field-marshal in the French army. Henry, the younger son, was created Grand Prior of France by King Louis XIV, though according to the diplomat Robert Wolseley he was 'a useless and debauched drunkard'.

Arabella's brother John had become the Duke of York's page and was one of the many lovers of Charles II's mistress Barbara Villiers. Arabella herself later married Sir Charles Godfrey, Clerk-Comptroller of the Green Cloth in the household of Charles II, with whom she settled down in Great Windmill Street. She had two further children and lived to be eighty-two.

The social life of the court was conducive to infidelity. Maids and pages, grooms and ladies acted as if they were one family of brothers and sisters whose duty was to serve their parent the King and to amuse themselves with each other. The incest barrier soon came between them, however, and their sexual interest in one another waned as fast as it waxed. But they never ceased needing to reinvigorate their passions, which were quickly resurrected by a change of partners.

Arabella's successor as James's mistress was Anne Hamilton, the daughter of the 1st Duke of Hamilton and a former mistress of Lord Chesterfield. This wealthy and witty woman, three years his junior, was James's lover for about seven years. She had married William Douglas, Earl of Selkirk – whom she successfully petitioned to be made Duke of Hamilton – only to leave him and 'pass through the hands of several other gentlemen'.

James had brief affairs with the sister of Sarah Jennings, the future Duchess of Marlborough, with Letitia Smith, who in 1657, after the affair with James, married Lord Robartes, and with Mary Bagot, widow of the Earl of Falmouth, who had been killed in 1665 at the Battle of Lowestoft, where James had commanded the English fleet. And in 1667 he was greatly attracted to Frances Stewart, a maid of honour of his wife. Frances was also ardently admired by Charles II, who failed to persuade her to become his mistress. She clearly found the idea of having to choose between the King and his brother too daunting, and quickly married the elderly Duke of Richmond, to whom she remained faithful.

Mary Kirke was the daughter of George Kirke, Groom of the Bedchamber to Charles II, and was herself a maid of honour to the Duchess of York. Her mother, who had been a bedchamber woman to Queen Henrietta Maria, was by no means a strict guardian, and in about 1674 Mary (or Moll) appears to have encouraged three lovers simultaneously: James Duke of York, his nephew the Duke of Monmouth and Lord Mulgrave. In 1675 the Duchess forced Mary to resign her position.

James's last mistress, Catherine Sedley, was the daughter of the notorious Sir Charles Sedley, courtier, poet, debauchee and wit. Her father had tried to buy John Churchill, Arabella's eldest brother, as his son-in-law, but John preferred the more attractive, but poorer, Sarah Jennings. Catherine was probably the most significant of all James's mistresses in that, though coarse and cruel, she was politically astute and had she wished she could have protected his reputation rather than undermining it. In a way, she was to James very much as Nell Gwyn was to Charles II – demanding nothing of him. And yet his association with her was to destroy his reputation.

Catherine was described by a one contemporary as 'skinny and squinted'; John Evelyn said she was 'none of the most virtuous, but a wit'. She is remembered for her comment on her apparent inability to explain James's desire for her: 'It cannot be my beauty for I have none; and it cannot be my wit for he had not enough to know that I have any.' It was most likely that James desired her in response to her declared need for him, which mitigated her lover's ever-present fear of rejection. She became James's mistress some time after 1678, when she became maid of honour to his elder daughter Mary. In 1680 she bore the Duke a daughter and in 1684 a son, James Darnley, who lived for just a year. When James became King, Catherine moved into the apartments in St James's Square previously occupied by Arabella Churchill, who by then had decamped with her husband.

Catherine was a devout and bigoted Protestant and lost no opportunity to denigrate Catholic doctrine. Her affair with James was encouraged by the pillars of the Established Church in the hope that she might influence him to deny his adopted religion. It was some time before James realized that his involvement with Catherine was being used for political purposes, and he then made half-hearted attempts to give her up. When these failed, he created her Countess of Dorchester to appease her.

When James had married Mary of Modena in 1673, the Queen was greatly upset by the favour shown to Catherine. Evelyn observed that 'for two dinners, standing near her, she hardly ate one morsel, nor spake one word to the King, or to any about her, who at all other times was used to be extremely pleasant, full of discourse and good humour'. Mary prompted the court priests to refuse to hear James's confession, and under this moral threat he agreed to give up his mistress, claiming that the creation of the Dorchester title had been a sop to get rid of her. He relapsed soon after, however, and Mary had to insist that Catherine be banished from the court – threatening to become a nun unless this was done. Catherine was persuaded to go to Ireland with a doubled stipend. But she hated it there and soon returned to England, though she was then received with less ardour than before from James.

Catherine later married the one-eyed Sir David Colyear, an officer in the army of William of Orange, later created Earl of Portmore. She bore him two sons, to whom she gave the advice 'If anybody call either of you the son of a whore you must bear it, for you are so. But if they call you bastards, fight till you die; for you are an honest man's sons.'

In February 1685, on the death of his brother Charles, the Duke of York acceded to the throne as James II. For the first six months of his reign he was greeted enthusiastically by the people, despite his declared Roman Catholicism. The 51-year-old King had inherited a loyal Tory parliament. But, not satisfied with the peaceful Protestant England left to him by his brother, perhaps to appease his conscience it was not long before he began to attempt a rearrangement of the rules concerning Catholics who had not accepted the authority of the Church of England and who, as a result, had been disadvantaged politically. The country had been looking forward to a period of prosperity with the King and Parliament working in harmony to uphold the dignity of the Crown. What had not been anticipated was James's attempt to reintroduce Roman Catholicism. Liberty of conscience was one thing, but a reverse discrimination against the national church was entirely unacceptable.

In June, James Scott, Duke of Monmouth, Charles II's son by his mistress Lucy Walter, took it upon himself to attempt the overthrow of the King with a sizeable army of Protestant peasantry. Monmouth was the oldest son of Charles II and had always thought of himself as his father's rightful heir, though, despite claims that his parents had married, there was no evidence one way or another as to his legitimacy. Monmouth was ultimately unsuccessful in his bid to overthrow his uncle, and James appointed Chief Justice Jeffreys to try the rebels. Executions and transportations became so commonplace that Jeffreys's courtroom was known as the 'Bloody Assizes'.

James's brief period of authority had undone all the good brought about by the Restoration. He had antagonized Parliament by his many Catholic appointments and by his alliance to Catholic France, and to make matters worse he produced a male heir by Mary of Modena, thus ensuring a Catholic succession, whereas Parliament had hoped that the throne would pass to the Protestant children of his first marriage, to Anne Hyde. In 1688 an approach was made to Prince William of Orange, the husband of James's daughter Mary, in the hope that he would save England from Catholicism. (Among those who supported this approach was Sir Charles Sedley, who took full advantage of the damage to James's reputation caused by the affair with his daughter, Catherine. He commented that King James had made his daughter a countess and he would repay the honour by making James's daughter Mary a queen.) William responded, and he and his troops were welcomed by most of the population when they landed near Torbay. The immature James's long-time fear of rejection was at last fulfilled and, though James was captured, William allowed him safe passage to France, where, after unsuccessful attempts to regain his throne, he died in September 1701.

4

William IV
Sailor King or 'Silly Billy'?

William Henry, the third son of King George III and Queen Charlotte, was born on 21 August 1765 at Buckingham House. Sixty-five years later he was crowned King William IV. As a young man it had rarely occurred to him that one day he might accede to a throne in which he was not particularly interested and to which he was in no way suited. He had two older brothers: George, Prince of Wales, who reigned after the death of their father in 1820 as the hugely overweight, morally dishonest George IV and whom William succeeded in 1830, and Frederick, Duke of York, who died in 1827 and whose sexual excesses probably exceeded even those of his older brother.

Until he was seven William shared a nursery with George and Frederick, but then his parents decided to take him away from the two older brothers he adored and moved him, with his younger brother Edward for company, to the former home of Lord Bute at Kew Green, not far from the royal residence at Kew Palace. Thereafter he spent his childhood virtually separated from his parents at a boarding-school where there was only one teacher, one other pupil and no holidays and where he was very formally taught. William and Edward lived in separate apartments and were brought up their governess, Lady Charlotte Finch. William experienced little in the way of love apart from the brief companionship of his elder brother George, whom he idolized.

King George and Queen Charlotte – the former Princess Charlotte of Mecklenburg-Strelitz – seemed to enjoy producing children but were unable to cope with the logistics of bringing them up. Their carefree attitude to parenting, and indeed to marriage itself, was probably due to the influence of the King's father, George II. When George II's wife, Queen Caroline, died of cancer in 1737 she begged him on her deathbed to marry again. He was then fifty-four. 'No, no,' he replied, 'I'll just have mistresses.' Unlike other royal children, before and since, who were brought up by attendants under parental guidance, Queen Charlotte's fifteen children were more or less left to their own devices. Only Princess Amelia, her last-born, would have seen her mother without a swollen abdomen.

Nearly all William's siblings were social misfits, and none of his brothers was suited to fulfil his royal destiny. Being brought up against a background of court etiquette which even by late-eighteenth-century standards was not only impersonal but inflexible, created fifteen rebellious individuals whose antisocial behaviour alarmed their contemporaries. In addition to the insatiable sexual demands that the Prince of Wales, the Duke of York and Prince William made of any women who crossed their paths, the King's fourth son, Edward, Duke of Kent, was a strong believer in vicious corporal punishment. While he was governor of Gibraltar he enjoyed flogging 'natives' who misbehaved. And Ernest Augustus, Duke of Cumberland, the fifth son, was a demagogue who possibly knew right from wrong but chose not to distinguish between them.

Before the rare and then undiagnosed genetic disorder porphyria resulted in a total breakdown in his mental functioning, George III tried in the early part of his sixty-year reign to bring up his children in the way that he himself had been raised. He and Queen Charlotte were dutiful but scarcely demonstrative. The King is said to have shown some fondness for their second son, Prince Frederick, and Prince William believed that his mother loved him. But such affection as there was was only relative and made little difference to the overall effect of the children's background on their social functioning.

The rigidity of their upbringing meant that the children were trained rather than reared, which was seen as appropriate to the expectations imposed on them by their royal destiny. None of William's brothers was permitted to sit in the presence of their mother, and when they walked in the gardens of their home at Kew they were expected to form a crocodile in pairs graded according to size. William was possibly the least affected by all this, possibly because he was the least sensitive to his surroundings. (He was later reported as habitually sleeping through the opera and being unable to recognize even the national anthem.) Nevertheless, his comments at his brother Frederick's funeral in 1827 say a great deal about his attitude to his parents. He was heard to tell his younger brother the Duke of Sussex not once but several times that 'We shall be treated *now* brother Augustus, very differently from what we have been.'

It was not until King George and Queen Charlotte were satisfied that they had produced sufficient potential heirs to allow for any mishaps that their strict domestic regime was relaxed. Their last few children – of no dynastic importance – benefited not so much from a hands-on intimacy as from a careless indifference to anything other than their physical well-being.

In the early days of his illness, before the deterioration in his mental state, George III was preoccupied with the importance of obedience and authority. He would have preferred to be an absolute monarch, but he respected the constitution and the legal obligation imposed upon him to share power with Parliament. However, his instinctive obstinacy and prejudice against reform of any kind made it difficult for him to assess the advice given to him by his ministers. His bigoted and fundamentalist view of Christianity, for example, as well as his insistence on absolute obedience from his subjects and his children, conflicted with the radical new ideas and changes that were beginning to germinate both in the outside world and even, albeit reluctantly, within himself.

King George never managed to resolve the conflict between his instinctive absolutism and a weak conscience-driven form of liberalism in what, for him, passed as family life. He allowed none of his children any right of expression. Their views, on the rare occasions when they were permitted to air them, were never taken into account. Neither were his children able to find maternal comfort in their mother Queen Charlotte. Tired and bewildered for the first twenty-two years of her marriage by almost perpetual pregnancy, the dull, withdrawn and probably mildly depressed mother of fifteen had no say whatsoever in the military routine of her children's lives. As run by the King, the family of the English branch of the House of Hanover was a dictatorship peopled by young men whose dissolute behaviour was ultimately to drive their well-meaning but misguided parents to despair.

When George III inspected the Channel Fleet anchored off Spithead in 1778 he was both thrilled and depressed. He was impressed by the smartly turned out officers and fit, alert young men ready to go to sea and highly trained to respond to danger; he was depressed because not one of his three eldest children could measure up to any of them. Standing on the deck of the *Prince George*, the ninety-gun flagship commanded by Admiral Augustus Keppel, the King could not have helped reflecting, not for the first time, on his fruitless efforts to turn his sons – noble princes of the blood royal and heirs to his throne – into men of whom he could be proud, instead of having to try to shut his eyes to their anarchic behaviour.

George III's life had been ruled by his submission to the authority under which he had been brought up, and he resented the fact that his elder sons were less docile. He had instructed the boys' tutors to thrash them for disobedience but to little effect, possibly because their father's views on punishment were untainted by mercy. He was particularly anxious about the poor example that George and Frederick were setting Prince William. He wanted to prevent him from developing into another badly behaved reprobate who would bring disgrace to the royal house. Gambling, sex and alcohol had already become the order of the day for his first two sons, but he determined not to allow the same to be true for William and felt it was not too late to encourage him along a path from which the other two had already strayed. If separated from his brothers, the thirteen-year-old prince could perhaps yet become a credit to him.

At a time when William was testing out his barely pubertal sexuality with one of his mother's maids of honour, the King hastily informed Captain Robert Digby (promoted at once to rear-admiral) that he wished his son to be enrolled into the Royal Navy and to be 'treated with civility but with no visible marks of respect'. William was in addition to be 'early taught obedience and to conduct himself with politeness'. Fine expectations perhaps, but, despite naval discipline and the efforts of the tutors responsible for his continuing education, the future King William IV (later referred to by monarchists as the Sailor King) was also known by those who knew him better as 'Silly Billy'.

King George continued to be disturbed by his adolescent third son's impulsiveness. He had always been irritated by William's habit of acting without thinking and was particularly aggrieved when, at home on leave one day, he left the drawing-room – almost in mid-sentence – to visit a brothel. The King, who could not bring himself to address his son personally on delicate issues such as sex, wrote to his tutor asking him to deal with the matter when William had returned to Portsmouth. William wrote back, 'I can assure you Sir, that I never did anything wrong when I left your Majesty.' As William had difficulty in distinguishing between right and wrong, however, the letter must be interpreted with this in mind.

At home again shortly after this, for his mother's birthday party at St James's Palace, William found himself drawn to Julia Fortescue, a girl of his own age, who lived with her parents in a grand house facing Green Park in London and who had only recently been presented at court. Julia and William – whose attitude to the court was less than reverential and who was looking to add some spice to what was otherwise a dull life – fell in love at first sight. Within days they were discussing marriage. The King was appalled. His sons would be permitted to marry only Protestant royalty, and he referred William to the 1772 Royal Marriages Act, which he had personally drawn up to prevent any member of the royal family under the age of twenty-five from marrying without the permission of the sovereign. Julia's parents were encouraged to remove their daughter to Scotland, and William had his leave cut short.

William took to the Navy, and the Navy took to him. This was partly because of the mix of respect due to royalty accorded to him by senior officers and the fact that he could behave as 'one of the boys' with his fellow cadets. Self-confident and outgoing, he was equally at home when on shore leave with his shipmates and when replying, in a speech written for him by his tutor, to the loyal toast on HMS *Victory* on the retirement of Admiral Sir Frances Geary in August 1780. He seldom took offence, and was as insensitive to criticism as he was to his father's expectations of him. He was not bullied, because he did not recognize bullying as such. He was as rowdy and aggressive as any of his shipmates and had no problem in holding his own in inebriated brawls in the midshipmen's mess. His major interests were sex, food and drink.

William enjoyed being in action and revelled in English successes against the French and Spanish fleets. He regarded naval warfare in the same light as he later regarded sex. He could not have been more elated when the Spanish fleet was engaged in battle – the senior officer on board the *Prince George*, Admiral Digby, wrote that 'the moment he saw [the Spaniards] were preparing for action his spirits rose to that degree that he was almost in a state of insanity' – but he became depressed when the engagement fizzled out. He was bored with his time spent learning mathematics and history, French and Latin, but aroused by the bloody backs of flogged deserters. His letters to his parents reflected his admiration for the harsh punishment inflicted on wrongdoers. He wrote to his father that 'there have been several Courts Martial upon deserters and mutinous people, most of who have been condemned to be flogged'. In a further letter, approving of what he had witnessed, he wrote, 'I have seen martial discipline kept up and the severity arising from it executed: the manner Courts Martial are held: the justice that is done in a free country.' Courts martial were an almost daily occurrence, and in a letter addressed to his mother congratulating her on her birthday he wrote somewhat insensitively, given the occasion, but certainly approvingly, of four men being sentenced to death for desertion.

William acquitted himself well in the engagements that followed the abortive battle of Cape St Vincent in January 1780. When the Spanish fleet was more fully engaged he was overheard shouting to a midshipman, 'Won't we give these haughty Dons a sound thrashing!' His first direct experience of the horrors of sea warfare came shortly afterwards, when he witnessed an explosion aboard the Spanish ship *Santo Domingo*, which sank with the loss of six hundred lives. This was followed by his whole-hearted involvement in drunken brawling in the streets and taverns of Gibraltar. Admiral Digby, turning a blind eye to William's high spirits while on shore leave, told his proud father that his son would make 'a very great sea officer'. London crowds welcomed the homecoming of the royal sailor, and his brothers celebrated by taking the over-excited William to wild parties in search of women.

His parents found to their dismay that William had picked up the shipboard vices of smoking, drinking and swearing. He had learned little of his shipmates' true feelings, since many concealed these behind flattery and unctuous fawning. His father had as yet no complaint to make about William's service record. But if he thought that life in the Navy would stamp out whatever tendency his son might have had to emulate his dissolute brothers he was to be disappointed. At home William imitated the behaviour of George and Frederick, and when on shore leave he led his fellow cadets into committing mayhem in the local taverns with an alcohol-driven enthusiasm comparable to that of the football hooligans of today.

King George was unimpressed with the social exploits of his son, and was relieved when William returned to his ship and to the naval discipline in which the King was beginning to lose confidence. William's parents wrote to him infrequently, and when they did their tone was admonitory and cold.

Approaching sixteen, Prince William was now beginning to show signs of the antisocial personality which later was to be manifested by his brother the Duke of Kent, whose sadomasochistic demands terrified the women with whom he came into sexual contact. His lack of concern for others, especially the young men who had infringed naval regulations and attracted brutal punishments, and his reckless, excitement-seeking behaviour, either with his brothers or with his fellow shipmates, shocked his parents. William was becoming more openly sadistic in his thinking. He wrote to his mother in 1780 to congratulate her on the birth of his brother Alfred, telling her with evident approval that, 'We have had Courts Martial held every day on board the *Prince George*. A man belonging to the *Foudroyant* was sentenced to receive 300 lashes for having struck his officers and four deserters from the *Valiant* were condemned to death.' Years later, after he had come to the throne, he unsuccessfully opposed the 1832 Reform Act designed to widen the franchise. William believed that only the aristocracy should have the vote. He never conformed to social norms when he could get away with not doing so. His sexual needs, though prodigious, were not those of Henry VIII, with his need to procreate, or those of Charles II, who usually demonstrated a concern for the welfare of his mistresses. Instead he used sexual activity both as an antidote to depression and as a means of acting out the violence generated within him by his mother's having been unable to satisfy his childhood needs.

Four years after William's enlistment, his father took the view that either the Navy was failing his son or his son was failing the Navy. He sent him to the court at Hanover for two years, to further his education and to have his courtly manners repolished. Neither of these two objectives was met. Prince William whiled away the agonizingly slow passage of time by consorting with prostitutes who were prepared to allow him to indulge his fascination with violence and punishment. There was little to amuse him in German court life, and he found it difficult to overcome his anti-German bigotry. He wrote to his friends that Hanover was boring and his Grand Tour of Europe's other courts even more so. He learned very little from what should have been a unique educational experience, and, when not looking for women, spent most of the time writing crude and angry letters to his brother George, complaining that those whom he had so far found were 'as poxied as whores'. He was well aware that many of the partners with whom he was involved suffered from sexually transmitted diseases, but he was prepared to gamble with his health to satisfy his craving for sexual satisfaction – just as he was prepared to spend night after night in gaming circles risking the meagre allowance provided for him by his father. On both counts he was a loser. He caught the 'pox' – probably herpes – from women, and he lost his money at the gaming tables. These losses were a not particularly subtle attack on his father, since it was he who was called upon to pay his son's debts.

Two years later, and with Hanover behind him, William was delighted to return to the Navy, where he was immediately promoted to lieutenant. When he eventually rose to command of his own ship, his father was disappointed when his son failed badly at the aspects of crew handling which would have marked him as a competent commander. William's early naval career was characterized by episodes of behaviour so inappropriate that it is difficult, other than by referring to his personality, to understand some of his actions. In 1786, at the age of twenty-one, having been appointed captain of the *Pegasus*, he was ordered to sail to the Caribbean. On the journey he became obsessed with discipline and enforced it with violent ruthlessness. His mood changes were so unpredictable that Sir Thomas Byam Martin, who was later to have a distinguished naval record, wrote that the Prince 'was deficient in almost all the qualities necessary for a person in high command'.

When the *Pegasus* docked in Halifax, Nova Scotia, William as usual spent much of his time in the local brothels. He also had a very public and indiscreet affair with Mrs Wentworth, the lesbian wife of the surveyor-general on the station – possibly seeing her indifference to heterosexuality as a challenge that it was his duty to overcome. He was increasingly exhibiting the classic split between affection and eroticism. So far there had been been little or no evidence that he actually liked women. He exploited them to satisfy his perverse sexual needs, but he rarely, if ever, showed them affection. It would be some time before he made his first faltering steps towards combining the two components of sexuality.

On his way home from Canada, William anchored in the south of Ireland, infuriating his father further not only by accepting the hospitality of leading Catholic families but also by his involvement with their Catholic daughters. Back in England and surprised to find that he was in disgrace once more, he decided that he would plead pressure of work and spend the Christmas and New Year of 1787–8 in Plymouth with his two older brothers, who had gone there to welcome him home. George and Frederick were overjoyed to see him, and the three of them lost no time in celebrating in the taverns and brothels of the town.

After Julia Fortescue's 'deportation' to Scotland, William had lost no time in finding replacements. Most of these had been prostitutes, but they no longer satisfied him. Once again at sea, he fell in love with the sixteen-year-old virginal daughter of a Spanish admiral in Cuba, and on this occasion he had to call upon Horatio Nelson to rescue him from the wrath of her family.

Prince William's eldest brother, George, Prince of Wales, had by now met and fallen in love with the devoutly Catholic Mrs Maria Anne Fitzherbert. Born Maria Smythe, a woman of respectable background, she was unlike any of the other women with whom George had been involved. Mrs Fitzherbert had been twice married and twice had experienced bereavement. At eighteen she had married Edward Weld of Lulworth Castle Dorset, a rich 44-year-old who died within a year after a fall from a horse. Three years later she had married her second husband, Thomas Fitzherbert, by whom she bore a son. Both her husband and her infant son died four years later in the South of France.

Mrs Fitzherbert was introduced to the Prince of Wales in 1785, at the opera, and he immediately began to court her. Refusing his advances on several occasions, she told him she would settle for nothing less than marriage. The Prince of Wales was so much in love that he would have agreed to anything and asked permission from his father to marry – only to be referred, like William before him, to the provisions of the Royal Marriages Act. However, George and Mrs Fitzherbert were married in secret by a bribed Church of England clergyman, the Reverend Robert Burt, behind locked doors in her drawing-room at Park Street in Mayfair on 5 December 1785. (George later repudiated the marriage in order to marry a Protestant princess and secure an heir to the throne.) Married in the eyes of God, Mrs Fitzherbert was not married in the eyes of the sovereign, and her official status remained that of mistress. But William had been given a sexual green light.

If his brother George could get away with philandering then so could William, and one woman after another responded to his charms, his status or his money. In 1790, having completed his education to the 'satisfaction' of his senior officers, Prince William retired from the Navy, only to be briefly recalled later in the year – albeit with some reluctance. Unsure of what to do with him next, in 1789 the King had created him Duke of Clarence and given him a stipend of £12,000 and a suite of rooms in St James's Palace, but nothing by way of useful purpose. Prevented from forming serious relationships with women whom he found attractive unless they were acceptable under the terms of the Royal Marriages Act, William resumed his associations with loose women.

In the spring of 1790, as he began to tire of the one-night stands that had previously satisfied his sexual needs, he met Dorothy Jordan, an actress said by her admirers to possess the most beautiful legs ever seen on the stage. Dorothy's parents, Francis Bland and Grace Phillips, had never married. Bland, an Irishman, was a stagehand in Dublin, though his ambition was to act. His father, a judge in the Prerogative Court in Dublin and a Doctor of Divinity, had already disinherited Francis's brother after he had become an actor and married an actress. Judge Bland considered the stage to be ungodly, disliked Grace Phillips and certainly disapproved of Francis's sexual involvement with her. In time, however, he came to accept their liaison and even provided them with a modest allowance.

Grace, though of Welsh extraction, was one of three sisters who had all made the stage their career in Ireland. The girls had been drawn to the theatre by watching classical plays performed by the many companies of strolling players who visited their home town of Bristol.

Grace's and Francis's daughter Dorothy was registered as having been born in Covent Garden in 1762, but most of her family lived in southern Ireland, in the countryside around Waterford. She was to have few happy memories of her childhood. When she was thirteen her father abandoned his family to marry an Irish actress in London, leaving Grace with their five children. Dorothy always said how much she hated Ireland, and she hated her father too – probably with good reason. She never forgot his turning his back on her or forgave him for it, and she spent the rest of her life seeking a replacement for him. As she grew older she often thought of how he had walked out on all of them with scarcely a goodbye. The fact that he had found another woman hurt her. At thirteen, she was just beginning to be in touch with her femininity and needed her father's approval. She did not want to have to compete for his love with another woman, particularly one who was not her mother. Until he died, in 1778, her memory of her father was kept alive by the meagre sums of money he sent to support his family.

Dorothy was well educated, and at fourteen, when she started work, she was sufficiently literate and numerate to hold down a job as an assistant in a Dublin milliner's. Her wages helped support her brothers and sisters. There had been no man in her life since her father had left the year before, but her looks were striking and it was not long before she acquired several admirers.

By the time her father died, Dorothy was already beginning to show some acting talent, and needed little persuasion by her mother to make the stage her career. In 1782 she joined a theatre company run by the Irish actor-manager Richard Daly. (Though afflicted with a squint, Daly was an expert duellist – allegedly because his strabismus made his opponents unable to tell if his aim was true until it was too late.) Dorothy became pregnant by Daly at the same time as his wife did and named her daughter Frances, after her father.

In competition for a father's love, once again Dorothy lost out. After a few months Daly abandoned her and returned to his wife. Dorothy crossed the Irish Sea with her mother and her four brothers and sisters to seek out an aunt in England who worked with the theatre company of actor-manager Tate Wilkinson. Like other men, Wilkinson was taken with Dorothy's looks, and after an impromptu audition in an inn he engaged her for fifteen shillings a week. Possibly referring to the crossing of the Red Sea and the fact she had 'crossed the water out of slavery', he gave her the stage name of Mrs Jordan. Dorothy's acting career now took off with her first performances in the provincial Yorkshire towns toured by his company.

It was not long before she became involved with another admirer. She was about seventeen when Charles Doyne, an army lieutenant, proposed marriage. Dorothy was attracted to him, but she was not yet ready to marry and, though she desperately needed to be loved, she was relieved when her mother refused permission. Her self-esteem was so low, however, that she had difficulty in refusing any man, and George Inchbald, the male lead in the Tate Wilkinson company, became her next lover. According to her biographer Claire Tomalin, she would have married him had he asked her, but he failed to do so until years later, after she had achieved fame on the London stage, when she turned him down.

In 1786 Dorothy met Sir Richard Ford, the son of a physician and an associate of the dramatist, theatre manager and MP Richard Brinsley Sheridan. Ford promised to marry her, and she moved into his home in Bloomsbury. Nothing came of his promise, however, other than three children: a boy, who died soon after birth, and two girls. Though the couple never married, Dorothy insisted on being known as Mrs Ford.

Her success on the stage brought her to the attention of Sheridan, who had already achieved fame with *The Rivals* and *The School for Scandal*, and Dorothy felt honoured that her acting ability was acknowledged by one of England's leading playwrights. She soon became his leading lady at the Drury Lane Theatre, of which he was part owner, making her début there with the lead role in *The Country Girl*.

Swiftly becoming the talk of the town, Dorothy was introduced to Prince William by Mrs Sheridan at one of the royal command performances, in which she received great acclaim. The meeting turned out well for all concerned. Mrs Sheridan was trying to rid herself of Prince William's attentions, Sheridan was pleased because the Prince gave up pursuing his wife soon after he met Dorothy, and Dorothy and Prince William were pleased because they took to one another.

There was one complication; Dorothy still regarded herself as married to Richard Ford – though she was not, and not even the realization that Prince William was attracted to his common-law wife gave Ford any interest in marriage. However, Dorothy and Ford now lived very close to William at Richmond, and this gave the Prince plenty of opportunity to persuade her to have an affair with him. Eventually – as always – she was unable to refuse.

Having finally made up her mind to leave Ford, Dorothy was unable to come to an agreement with him about which of them should have custody of their two children. After much discussion, they decided that Dorothy should buy a home for them, where they would be looked after by one of her sisters, and that all the expenses would be met by Ford.

Prince William's many affairs had previously been of little public interest, but when it was realized that he and 'Mrs Jordan' were planning to live together a sensational press storm ensued, with satirists such as Cruikshank and Gillray venting their indignation in daily cartoons. But both Dorothy and the Prince were determined to make their relationship work. William had calmed down considerably since meeting Dorothy – a mother *par excellence* – and he seemed genuinely to love her. There was nothing Dorothy would not do for the Prince, and, though her involvement was driven by her ongoing need for a father, she became the 'mother' he would have liked to have had. Their emotional needs fitted together harmoniously.

The couple had several homes before finally settling into domestic bliss at Bushy Park, a mansion near Richmond, where in January 1794 George, the first of their ten children, was born. The scandal that surrounded them gradually subsided, probably because more pressing issues such as war and political unrest filled the newspapers. Mrs Jordan, who was still on the stage, involved herself in charitable works, while William did his best to discharge his many debts by playing at farming.

Their idyllic life away from the public gaze began to wind down in 1806, when the political muckraker William Cobbett attacked the royal family and their hangers-on in a series of articles in his *Weekly Political Register*. A few

years later, at the time of the regency in 1810, Prince William's elder brother
George encouraged him to think carefully of his position, especially his
financial one, since Parliament would vote more money to a married prince
than to one living in sin with ten bastard children. As the royal family had
fallen deeply into debt, this was not a consideration to be dismissed lightly,
and in 1811 William left Mrs Jordan. The final push had come from his
mother, and William was so amazed that she had at last taken an interest in
his welfare that he readily agreed with her suggestion that the time had come
for him to marry. (The effect on Dorothy's looks and figure of her fifteen
illegitimate children in twenty-five years may also have had something to
do with his agreement.) As accommodating as ever, Dorothy accepted
William's decision. She was easily persuaded that he had to find a rich
princess and provide himself with an heir lest one day he should be called
upon to play a more important role in the affairs of the country.

William had been generous during their relationship, but he had also
depended on Dorothy's money, for her acting career was more successful
than his naval one. A contemporary satirical rhyme went:

> As Jordan's high and mighty squire
> Her playhouse profits deigns to skim,
> Some folks audaciously enquire
> If he keeps her or she keeps him.

Dorothy had been a loyal and loving partner to William for sixteen years,
and understood that he was virtually bankrupt. In 1811 she left her house
and their children without a word of reproach. Three years later she retired
from the stage, and in the following year she went to live in in the village of
Saint-Cloud in the Hauts-de-Seine in France. William had agreed to a
financial settlement, but he soon reneged on it and, having supported many
members of her extended family in Ireland as well as her live-in partner,
Dorothy died in poverty in 1816.

Denied the level of paternal love that she believed was her due –her itin-
erant father was seldom at home even before he left altogether – Dorothy
had sought compensatory admiration not only from audiences but also from

father figures. The most exalted of these was the future sovereign, the father of his people. It took Dorothy twenty years to discover that repeatedly trying to turn men into her father provided at best a delusion and at worst a repetition of the paternal neglect to which she had been exposed.

Once rid of his loyal and loving mistress, William was ready to marry. But he had great difficulty in finding a suitable princess foolish enough to take him on. His reputation had gone before him, and no one seemed to want an involvement with a sex addict whose need to act out his violent fantasies with prostitutes was common knowledge. Others suspected that his mental state made him difficult to live with, despite the evidence to the contrary while he was with Dorothy. Eventually, in 1818, Princess Adelaide of Saxe-Meiningen agreed to become his bride. She proved unable to provide him with an heir, however. Her first two daughters died in infancy, and subsequent twin daughters were stillborn.

Regarded as a buffoon not only by his political enemies but also by his family and friends, William probably suffered from what would now be called bipolar mood disorder. His mood swings ranged from depression to uncontrollable hyperactivity. He craved excitement to counter the downside to his nature and also abused alcohol as a stimulant when his mood was low. When he was high he became irrational and unmanageable, his speech was pressured, he was impulsive and extravagant, and his sexual needs were exaggerated. His mood was seldom stable.

William spent his life scapegoating women. He turned his back on one after another, wreaking sexual and emotional havoc in the process. Not until Dorothy Jordan loved him for himself and played the role of mother ten times over did he finally find happiness. Hostility triumphed, however, and he abandoned Dorothy just as his mother had abandoned him. Having learned to live with rejection since she was thirteen, Dorothy accepted William's leaving her as being no more than she could expect.

One of Prince William's first acts on accession to the throne in 1830, on the death of his brother George without an heir, was to agree to pay Francis Chantrey 2,000 guineas to execute a life-size sculpture depicting a woman cradling two infant children, which the King intended to place in Westminster Abbey. The face of the statue was to be taken from the many likenesses of

Mrs Jordan, who had died fourteen years earlier, and the children were to represent her and the Prince's eldest son (in 1831 created Earl of Munster) with his baby brother. The new King reportedly wept as he gave Chantrey the commission. Because of opposition by the Church, however, the statue never made it to the abbey. It languished for over a hundred years in a series of private gardens before being given to Queen Elizabeth II. It now stands – a belated monument to minimalist remorse – in the gardens of Buckingham Palace.

5

Edward VII

Rien Ne Va Plus

The future Edward VII, grandson of the Duke of Kent, the fourth of King George III's disreputable sons, was brought up in the hope that he would not perpetuate the excesses of the House of Hanover. Only too aware of the danger of such a heritage, however, Edward's parents relied on strict tutelage rather than a sensitive awareness of their son's needs to ensure that he would grow up with a sense of self-worth. In the event, when he came to adulthood, the insecure and unloved Prince sought comfort from one woman after another for the love denied him as a child.

In 1819, when she was six months old, Edward's mother, the then Princess Victoria, was on holiday with her parents in Sidmouth, a seaside town in Devon. Within a week of their arrival her father, the Duke of Kent, developed a cough which was diagnosed as pneumonia. Four weeks later (despite cupping and bleeding) the Duke was dead. His wife, Princess Victoria of Saxe-Coburg-Saalfeld, never remarried, and their daughter Victoria, deprived of a father, came to rely on other older men for wisdom and support.

Victoria's childhood was not a happy one. She was both sad and angry, and probably regarded it as her mother's fault that she grew up with no man to whom she could appeal to right her wrongs, no male advocate to represent her interests if she were ever unjustly treated. At eighteen, having become Queen when her uncle William IV died without a legitimate heir, she resented her mother's friendship with Sir John Conroy, a married Irish army officer who had been appointed controller of her mother's household after the death of her father, and with whom her mother was rumoured to be having an affair. Wounded that her mother seemed to have more time for

Conroy than for her daughter, Victoria's first act on acceding to the throne was to banish Sir John from the court.

Still resentful at what she considered to be her mother's infidelity both to her and to the memory of the father she had never known, Victoria then found an opportunity both to spite her mother and, at the same time, to blacken Conroy's name. Conroy was seen driving in a carriage with one of the Queen's ladies-in-waiting, the unmarried but apparently pregnant Lady Flora Hastings. The Queen insisted that the woman be medically examined, but her physician found Lady Hastings to be virgo intacta and declared that her swollen abdomen was due to a malignant tumour. When her poor lady-in-waiting died some months later, the Queen was humiliated, which led her to feel more unloved than ever. Her feelings of low self-esteem persisted and were only minimally assuaged by a number of older men such as the 58-year-old Prime Minister, Lord Melbourne, and her uncle Prince Leopold of Belgium, who took it upon themselves to act as surrogate fathers.

Prince Leopold was quick to see the political benefits of a match between his niece Victoria and his nephew Prince Albert, the younger son of his brother Ernst, Duke of Saxe-Coburg-Saalfeld. Victoria had first met her cousin Albert when he and his brother had visited London in 1836 and had then been no more impressed with him than she had been with any of the other male cousins who had been presented to her. She did not see Albert again for three years, when, possibly to his surprise, the more mature Victoria fell madly in love with him.

In 1840, both aged twenty, they married and found in each other their other halves. The dysphoric Albert had seldom been happy during his childhood. When he was four years old his mother, Louise, daughter of the Duke of Saxe-Gotha-Altenburg, had left his father for the Count von Polzig-Baiersdorf and, having been banished from the court, had gone to live in Switzerland. Earlier her name had been linked with a Jewish court chamberlain who was rumoured to be Albert's biological father.

Like Victoria, Albert had grown up in a single-parent family. As a child he had no idea why he no longer had a mother and blamed both his father for her absence and his mother for abandoning him. When he agreed to marry Victoria he was only too pleased to escape from a motherless childhood which had brought him nothing but unhappiness and was delighted to have the Queen of England, the mother of her people, in love with him. Albert had grown up to be obsessed with the evils of illicit sex and spent much of his later life providing his son, the future King Edward VII, with an education designed to protect him against 'moral turpitude'. It was therefore probable that, as soon as he was old enough to do so, his son would turn to the compensations of wine, women and money to counterbalance the strictures and emotional inadequacies of his upbringing.

By November 1841, when Prince Edward was born, Queen Victoria had already given birth to a daughter with whom both she and Prince Albert were besotted. Having been deprived of a mother for most of his life, Albert looked to his wife and daughter to love him. Princess Victoria – their beloved 'Pussy', later known as Vicky – could do no wrong. In contrast, Prince Edward, the Prince of Wales, could do no right. He had been a large baby at birth, and the exhausted Queen, apparently either not feeling or ignoring any need to bond with him, was only too pleased to hand 'the boy', as she called him, over to a wet nurse, Mrs Roberts. Six weeks were to pass before Victoria asked for her son to be brought to her for a brief visit. His mother was seldom to refer to Edward by name thereafter. The heir to the throne remained 'the boy', unidentified and barely acknowledged by his mother until he left home at eighteen.

Prince Edward spent most of the cold winter of 1841–2 in Buckingham Palace, contemplating the wallpaper in a nursery several hundred yards of chilly corridors away from his mother. It was his misfortune that he was a placid baby who demanded little attention from the nursery staff. Like other 'good' babies, he therefore missed out on the essential stimulation that 'bad' babies attract. It was not long before he became aware that his pretty, vivacious older sister was his parents' favourite. By the time his younger sister Alice – affectionately nicknamed 'Fat Alice' – was born in 1843 Edward had developed such a vacuum of need that, despite his best efforts to fill it with the love of one woman after another – many of them married and themselves mothers – for the rest of his life he remained addicted to emotional input of every kind.

Edward was nineteen when he first discovered the delights of sex. In

1861 he had been sent for military training with the Grenadier Guards at the Curragh in Ireland. There, after a drunken party, he was introduced by some brother officers to Nellie Clifden, a camp follower, an aspiring actress and an amateur prostitute. The fact that Edward had to buy her love did not bother him. He was used to it. As a child he had never been loved unconditionally, and he was accustomed to rewarding his parents in one way or another for their limited approval.

Edward continued to see Nellie on his return to London, but his enjoyment of their relationship was short-lived. When he resumed his studies at Cambridge, a possibly well-meaning fellow officer informed Prince Albert of his son's indiscretion. Despite a feverish illness, Albert insisted on travelling to the university to express his outrage at Prince Edward's behaviour. He told him that his son had inflicted on him 'the greatest pain I have yet felt in this life'. Two weeks later, on 14 December, Prince Albert was dead.

Though typhoid fever – for which Edward could have in no way been responsible – was the official cause of death, the Queen had no doubt as to the true reason. Her son had killed his father by his 'disgusting' behaviour. She wrote to her eldest daughter that 'I never can or shall look at him without a shudder', and she never forgave her son for his behaviour or ceased to remind him of it. Edward – unloved as a child, his self-esteem already dangerously low and now ostracized by his mother – became drawn to others whose need for acceptance and approval matched his own.

Like many actresses, Nellie Clifden looked to the stage as a means to fulfil her need for approval. The role of mistress to the heir to the throne was a part she could not refuse. Like Prince Edward she, too, was nineteen, and she was unable to play the most important role of her career without boasting of her achievement to her friends. Prince Edward was equally indiscreet. For these two high-profile players, it was not so much that all the world was a stage but that all the world was an audience. Nellie was the first of many to be auditioned for the role of Edward's mistress.

Nellie had grown up in rural Ireland and was ambivalent about the English presence in her impoverished country. A young romantic, she was empowered not so much by the intimacy of her relationship with the heir to the British throne as by the fantasy that she had been chosen to strengthen the ties between her country and his. The eldest son of King Henry VII, Prince Arthur, had some 350 years earlier claimed to have been 'in Spain' after his supposedly unconsummated wedding night with Catherine of Aragon. It is unlikely that Nellie would have wondered whether Prince Edward believed himself to have been 'in Ireland' on the night *their* relationship was consummated. They would have been more carried away by the moment than with wondering whether increased Anglo-Irish understanding might have arisen out of their passionate embrace, and they never saw one another again after the death of Prince Albert.

In the first months of her bereavement and expecting that she would soon be joining her beloved Albert, Victoria was insistent that her son's life be brought under control and the succession be assured before she died. She chose as his wife, and her successor, his fourth cousin, Alexandra, an eighteen-year-old Danish princess, whom Edward then fell in love with. He knew that he was neither ready for the responsibility of marriage nor even fully grown up, but the idea of having an ever-ready sex partner who was outgoing, sociable, full of fun and also pretty was hard to resist. Both before and after their betrothal, in September 1862, Princess Alexandra and Prince Edward were seldom alone together for longer than a discreet peck on the cheek. Alexandra, however, was so enamoured and so excited that Queen Victoria had deemed her suitable for her heir that – had protocol not forbidden it – she might well have become mistress number two.

Alexandra was the daughter of Prince Christian of Denmark, who, when his older brother formed a morganatic marriage, in 1863 eventually acceded to become King Christian IX. Compared with the hardships that Edward had had to endure, Alexandra's childhood was idyllic. Her parents were warm and accepting of her natural exuberance, and her lifestyle was simple. She was tall and elegant, and after her marriage in 1863 she became a trendsetter for English women. She spoke French and German, as did Edward, but her English was poor. This was not a problem, however, because their relationship was largely physical. The only drawback was Alexandra's impaired hearing, but, since no one had listened to Edward as a child, the fact that his wife could not hear what he said did not trouble him – though it may possibly have contributed to the booming voice which he adopted on formal occasions.

Marlborough House, their home, close to Buckingham Palace, came to be associated with wit, culture, wealth and glamour, and the parties held there were legendary. Edward and Alexandra danced and laughed, and society danced and laughed with them. But in 1870, when Alexandra was twenty-six years old, the rheumatic fever which had complicated her sixth and final pregnancy affected her knee, and the dancing abruptly stopped. Edward, already a known habitué of French brothels, now became more open in his search for recreational sex.

Paris in the 1870s must have seemed to Edward to be the sexual epicentre of the universe. There was no diversion money could not buy. The most beautiful courtesans were drawn to him, and members of the *demi-monde* fought with one another for the privilege of his company. The Prince was so aroused by the number of women who swore they loved him that for several years the austere coldness of his childhood was mitigated by the warm glow of bars and brothels. His lifestyle did not adversely affect his image, and the French sex industry was given the 'royal seal of approval' by the grandeur of his presence.

Edward was not one to keep his feelings to himself. He wrote love-letters to his mistresses, and his money spoke eloquently to them. His favoured brothel was La Chabanais, and his favourite mistress Mme Giulia Barucci – who, with honest pride in her work, described herself as 'the greatest whore in the world'. Unfortunately for Edward, when Mme Barucci died from tuberculosis in 1871 it was found that she had kept all his more than indiscreet letters. Her brother blackmailed him with them, and eventually, following prolonged negotiations, Edward agreed to buy them back for £240, a sum he considered exorbitant.

Another mistress, though scarcely unique to him, was the singer Hortense Schneider. So popular was she with several other male members of Queen Victoria's extended family that she was known as 'Le Passage des Princes'.

In his early philandering days Edward's women were, like himself, heavily attracted to gratification. They were pleased with his money, and he was pleased with their attention to his needs. He had switched from the narcissistic over-concern for the self that characterizes the lonely child to the hands-on gratification he paid women to provide. It was but a step from the sexual role-play of the stars of the brothel, where audience participation heightened the enjoyment, to the drama of the theatre, where the audience paid to observe the actors from a respectful distance.

In the mid-1870s, tiring of prostitutes and their games and aspiring to a different arena, Edward became interested in the theatre. At least two of his mistresses were actresses whose skills appealed to the theatre-going public, ensuring them of an immortality that perhaps Edward one day hoped to share. He was drawn more than ever to those who, like him, needed to be admired, and in 1877 he was formally introduced to the beautiful actress Mrs Lillie Langtry, née Emilie Charlotte Le Breton.

Emilie Le Breton was born on 13 October 1853 in the Old Rectory, St Saviour, Jersey, the last but one of seven children and the only girl. As with other upper-class girls of the time, she was educated at home with a governess and later by her brothers' tutors. Her father was the Very Reverend William Corbet Le Breton, Dean of Jersey. He was exceptionally tall and handsome and looked every inch a soldier. (A general is said to have remarked on first meeting him, 'Do you know, sir, that when you joined the Church there was a deuced fine sergeant major spoilt!') Emilie's mother, the former Emilie Davis Martin, was small and fragile and not unlike Queen Victoria in appearance. Charles Kingsley once described her as 'the most bewitchingly beautiful creature' he had ever seen.

Le Breton had little time for any of his children. And, unlike Edward's father, the austere and sexually apathetic Prince Albert, the Dean was a 'ladies' man'. The 'lower classes' of Jersey blamed Le Breton for the frequency with which his distinctive features appeared among the next generation and the contribution to this phenomenon presumably made by their wives and daughters. When at the age of sixteen Emilie fell in love with a boy slightly younger than she, her father discouraged the relationship and had eventually to admit that the boy was his illegitimate son. Two of his 'upper-class' parishioners – a colonel and an admiral – once set upon him with their walking-sticks outside a Jersey church because he had left, after the service, with their beautiful wives, one on each arm. Leaving the women to explain themselves, Le Breton beat a retreat. The encounter did little for his dwindling reputation.

Headstrong, tomboyish and competitive with her brothers, Emilie was more at home with boy's games than with those associated with Victorian girls. Believing that her brothers received more attention than she did, she often wished that she was a boy. As a child of eleven she once ran naked down a Jersey street after dark because her older teenage brothers had dared her to do so.

Her exploited and neglected mother had found her own way of dealing with her husband's indiscretions. She simply went to bed with frequent and unexplained illnesses and shut her eyes to the problem. Emilie, however, was determined not to be a doormat. With a sexually grandiose and largely absent father and a weak and frightened mother, she decided that the dysfunctional family home had little to offer. In 1874, at the age of twenty-one, and with the grudging consent of her parents, she married Edward Langtry, widower of another Jersey beauty, Jane Price.

Langtry, plump, and interested only in sailing and fishing, was the wealthy grandson of a self-made shipping magnate. He told Emilie that he had taken a law degree at Oxford but had never practised. She was probably interested more in his magnificent sailing yacht, *Red Gauntlet*, than in Langtry himself. 'One day', she said, 'there came into the harbour a most beautiful yacht. I met the owner and fell in love with the yacht. To become the mistress of the yacht I married the owner, Edward Langtry.'

Emilie was soon deeply disappointed not only with the yacht but also with her husband. Much of the first year of their married life was spent not in London, as she had imagined it would be, but in Jersey, where they were married, or on *Gertrude*, another of the Langtry yachts. Edward made it clear that he had no intention of leaving the coast and his home, Cliffe Lodge, overlooking Southampton Water, to live in a landlocked metropolis. He was duller, less amenable to change and far less wealthy than Emilie had at first believed. He was also lazy, without curiosity or ambition, and they had nothing in common. Emilie and Edward began to live separate lives. Bored by her husband's yachting companions, Emilie ached for London society.

After a bout of typhoid fever in 1876, a year after their wedding, Emilie was advised by a doctor to convalesce in London, and the couple moved to an apartment in Eaton Place, Belgravia. A year later a chance meeting with

Lord Ranelagh, an old acquaintance from Jersey and a noted roué, led to an invitation to the home of Lady Sebright at 23 Lowndes Square. It was Emilie's first official London appearance. From then on she was never without admirers and soon became one of the most sought-after guests in town.

Fellow Jerseyman John Everett Millais used her as his model for Effie Deans in his painting of a scene from *The Heart of Midlothian*, which he entitled *A Jersey Lily* – after the flower she held in her hand, though this was apparently later identified as a Guernsey lily – the painting was exhibited in a gallery in St James's. Emilie reinvented herself as Lillie Langtry – the idea of being a flower did not appeal to her – and with her extraordinary looks and boyish wit she drew Pre-Raphaelite artists and avant-garde writers and poets to her door. Frank Miles, whose sketch of her was sold to a printer and mass-reproduced within days of their meeting, and James Whistler asked her to pose for them, and Oscar Wilde insisted on meeting her.

Wilde could not have been more impressed. He lauded her praises to everyone, and there was much speculation that he might have succumbed to her boyish charms. 'Lillie's beauty has no meaning,' he declared. 'Her charm her wit and her mind – what a mind! – are far more formidable weapons.' He and Whistler were both devoted to her. Millais was equally effusive, declaring, 'Lillie Langtry happens to be, quite simply, the most beautiful woman in the world.' However, he also said that Lillie was the most exasperating subject he had ever painted. For fifty minutes of each hour she looked only beautiful, but for the other ten she looked amazing. By 1878 Lillie had become a professional beauty, posing for photographs that would be hand-tinted and sold to the growing ranks of middle-class collectors.

At about this time Prince Edward gradually became drawn into a web that Lillie wove around her, designed to trap even the most wary visitor. A month after Lillie had been first discovered by Lord Ranelagh, on 24 May 1877 she and her husband were introduced to the Prince at a prearranged after-opera supper party given by the Arctic explorer Sir Allen Young at his home in Stratford Place. Sir Allen's home was frequently used by Edward and his brother Prince Alfred, the Duke of Edinburgh, as a place to meet their actress friends. (Lord Rosebery, another close friend, whom in 1892

Edward was to persuade to become Foreign Secretary in Gladstone's fourth ministry, had refused a request from Edward's private secretary to provide a similar service, as his house was 'too small'.) Edward was attracted by Lillie's upbringing, which he mistakenly believed had been warm and close. It seemed to have been the opposite to his own, though it was in fact similar. For her part, aware that beauty was only skin deep, the unloved Lillie knew that she needed more than her appearance to be assured of being accepted by society. She didn't know that behind Edward's braids and epaulettes lurked equally low levels of self-esteem.

In 1878 Lillie was presented to Queen Victoria, who looked straight ahead at the presentation and barely acknowledged her presence. But this formal recognition, grudging though it was, gave the 25-year-old Lillie an entrée into London society. Wherever she went, her beauty made her the centre of attention, and it soon became common knowledge in aristocratic circles that she was Prince Edward's mistress.

Soon after the beginning of Lillie's affair with the Prince, she and her husband moved to a new apartment in Norfolk Street, behind Park Lane. But Langtry's fortune – eaten away by his yachts – was insufficient to cover the upkeep of their new home, and within weeks he was bankrupt. For the first time since Lillie had left home with high hopes of a new life, she found herself with little or no money.

Her friends rallied round with suggestions for work, none of which appealed to her. Prince Edward was intermittently generous with monetary gifts, but they were not sufficient to maintain her lifestyle. He did, however, have a house built for her in Bournemouth – probably more in his interest than in hers – well away from prying London eyes, where he vainly hoped they could have assignations which would be known to only the two of them. And though Lillie's increasing celebrity had provided her with funds from portrait sittings and photographs, they were insufficient for her to furnish her new Bournemouth home in the style she wished. Edward had been cautious about taking married women as mistresses since his involvement in the 1870 Mordaunt divorce scandal had resulted in a good deal of public disapproval. In an emotional state after giving birth to a premature son, Lady Mordaunt had confessed to her husband that Prince Edward was the baby's

father. Two men were cited as co-respondents in the subsequent divorce proceedings, and Edward was subpoenaed as a witness. He robustly denied ever
having laid hands on her. The judge believed him, and Sir Charles Mordaunt lost the case on the grounds of his wife's insanity. Despite the need to
preserve his reputation, however, Edward paid regular incognito visits to
Lillie, and she visited him at Marlborough House.

Demoralized, defeated and with sexual activity in abeyance after the
move to Norfolk Street, Edward Langtry took to the bottle. He may also
have filed a petition for divorce in 1879, but if he did it was soon withdrawn.
There was no divorce and no scandal, and both Princess Alexandra and
Edward Langtry were forced to accept their partners' liaison. Langtry, on the
way to becoming an alcoholic, simply faded from the picture.

Oscar Wilde saved the day by encouraging Lillie to become an actress.
The idea of rapturous applause appealed to her, but unlike Sarah Bernhardt,
who had attended the Paris Conservatoire and who Lillie suspected was
waiting patiently in the wings to take her place as Edward's mistress, she had
had no formal stage training and was terrified of failure. Wilde introduced
her to Henrietta Labouchère, whose husband was a radical Member of Parliament and editor of *Truth*. An actress herself, Mrs Labouchère did what she
could to teach Lillie the rudiments of her craft, and some time later her pupil
was asked to take part in an amateur dramatic production at Twickenham.
Lillie's name was a box-office draw, and her new career was launched.

As a result of Henrietta Labouchère's training, Lillie successfully auditioned for the part of Kate Hardcastle in *She Stoops to Conquer*. She made her
West End début at the Haymarket Theatre in December 1881 and was an
immediate sensation. She was the first society woman to act on the English
stage, and the production was a success. Though some critics may not have
taken her seriously at first, the audiences did, and offers of other parts soon
followed. Her most successful role was Rosalind in *As You Like It*. Prince
Edward attended all her opening nights, even though he was beginning to
tire of her, and with his support she never looked back. She was popular not
only on the London stage but also in the provinces, and on one occasion she
toured the United States.

Wilde so admired Lillie that in 1893 he wrote his first play, *Lady Winder-*

mere's Fan, specially for her. Worried that she was too young to play the mother of a grown-up daughter – Lillie was then thirty-nine – Wilde amended the script to have her say, 'Besides, my dear Windermere, how on earth could I pose as a mother with a grown-up daughter? I have never admitted that I am more than twenty-nine, or thirty at the most. Twenty-nine when there are pink shades, thirty when there are not.' Shortly before Wilde's death on 30 November 1900 he said, 'The three women I have admired most are Queen Victoria, Sarah Bernhardt and Lillie Langtry – I would have married any one of them with pleasure.'

As Lillie's relationship with Edward had begun to fade, she had started an affair with his cousin Prince Louis Battenberg. This resulted in the secret birth of a daughter, Jeanne Marie Langtry, in Paris on 8 March 1881. On admitting the affair, Battenberg was sent back to the Navy by his irate family. Within three years he married Victoria, the daughter of Edward's late sister, Princess Alice, and it was this marriage that introduced the Mountbatten family (later to include Lord Louis Mountbatten of Burma, the youngest child of Prince Louis and Victoria, and later still Prince Philip, Duke of Edinburgh) to the royal scene. Lillie's world, however, had come crashing down.

Having lived beyond her means and those of her husband for many years, she could no longer stave off her creditors. Bailiffs eventually moved into the Norfolk Street house, and Lillie fled to Jersey with her infant baby, leaving her to be brought up by her mother. She brought her back to London in 1885, passing her off as her niece. It was only many years later that Jeanne learned that the woman whom she had been led to believe was her aunt was in fact her mother.

Though Prince Edward's affair with Lillie had cooled completely – probably because he had no wish to compete with her many other admirers – he still had loving feelings toward her and kept in touch with affectionate letters or visits. In 1899, two years after the death of Edward Langtry, Lillie married for the second time. Her new husband was the wealthy Hugo de Bathe, who became a baronet in 1907. Lillie's last stage appearance was in 1917. She died of a heart attack in Monte Carlo in 1929 at the age of seventy-six and was buried on Jersey, in the churchyard of St Helier parish church.

Edward had met Sarah Bernhardt briefly in Paris in the mid-1870s, but their affair probably began in 1879, when she visited London with the Comédie-Française. The 35-year-old actress provoked Lillie Langtry's sarcastic comment that 'with that [big] chin, she will go far', and Lady Frederick Cavendish described her equally unfairly as 'a woman of notorious, shameless, character'.

Sarah had become known as an elegant young woman of easy virtue who lived in the parish of Nôtre Dame de Lorette with her only child, Maurice, the result of a brief affair with Henri, Prince de Ligne, in 1863. Later stories that Edward was the child's father are certainly untrue, as Maurice was in his teens when Sarah and the Prince of Wales first met, though, never having known a father herself, Sarah was doubtless keen to invent one.

Sarah, born Henriette Rosine Bernhard in Paris in 1844, was the illegitimate daughter of Judith van Horn, a Dutch Jewish courtesan who worked in Paris as a milliner. Her putative father, Edouard Bernhard, was a law student. He provided for his mistress and her daughter for a time, but effectively disappeared from their lives when Sarah was about four years old. Sarah was educated at a local convent. With a childhood history which included not only an absentee father but also memories of other men who had become between her and her mother she decided, not unreasonably, that she wanted to become a nun. Charles, Duc de Morny, a half-brother of Napoleon III and her mother's lover, persuaded the sixteen-year-old that she would find her true *métier* in the theatre, and in 1860 he paid for Sarah to enter the Conservatoire in Paris to train as an actress.

By the time she first met Edward Sarah had had many relationships with men but had made a commitment to none of them. She feared intimacy and ran away from anyone who proposed it. She neither trusted men nor liked them, but that did not prevent her from embarking on a lifelong search for the 'father' whom she could scarcely remember. She was drawn more and more to roles in which she did not need to act but could simply be herself: the sexual victim, the mistress, the wronged woman. Victorien Sardou, one of the leading dramatists at the time who specialized in bourgeois drama, understood Sarah's needs. He created roles specially for her, and she became one of the most sought-after actresses of her day.

During the Comédie-Française's 1879 London season Edward paid

Sarah a great deal of attention. He reserved a box for each of her opening nights and was happy to have her received in society, often 'entertaining' her himself at Marlborough House until the early hours of the morning. Far from being dressy and curvaceous like Lillie Langtry, Sarah Bernhardt was thin, angular, bohemian and given to fashions that were provocative and revealing. Not least of her 'scandalous' ways were that she painted her face, lined her eyes with kohl, dyed her frizzy hair and even rouged her ear lobes. Her appearance was very different from anything that Edward had been used to.

Sarah was an obviously beautiful woman with the silken voice and deportment of an actress. Edward was much taken with her and once appeared with her on stage as 'the corpse' in Sardou's *Fedora*, in a scene in which the heroine, played by Sarah, weeps over the body of her murdered lover. His role required no acting skill, and he was not recognized.

Sarah, however, was a bird of passage. Her career was more important to her than her relationship with Edward, a 'father' who was as insubstantial as the one who had abandoned her as a baby. She was not unhappy to leave the field to Lillie Langtry, who was some nine years younger. All three of them were fond of practical jokes which inevitably discomforted their victims. Given the painful upbringing which they shared, this was not surprising. Edward himself played 'sexual' jokes on the hapless partners of his mistresses who were not amused.

Daisy, Lady Warwick, became Edward's mistress in 1886, after his long and passionate affair with Lillie Langtry and his brief liaison with Sarah Bernhardt. Born Frances Evelyn Maynard, at Easton Lodge, near Dunmow, Essex, in 1861, she was some eight years younger than Lillie and seventeen years younger than Sarah.

Daisy had no memory of her father, the Honourable Charles Maynard, who died when she was three years old. He was in fact a big, red-haired, blue-eyed colonel of the Blues, distinguished for his bravado, quick temper and addiction to alcohol. A superb horseman, he once leaped over the barrier at a bullfight in Spain, vaulted on to the bull's back and galloped the animal around the ring. He was the only son and heir of the third Viscount Maynard, who died, aged ninety-nine, three months after his son. When the will was read the Maynard family were disgusted and threw pats of butter at the portrait of the old Lord Maynard. His granddaughter Daisy was the sole legatee of a fortune that today would yield an annual income of around £750,000.

Daisy's mother, Blanche Maynard, née Fitzroy, was of royal descent. Her family could be traced back to Charles II both through the Duke of St Albans – King Charles's illegitimate son with his mistress Nell Gwyn – and the Duke of Grafton – King Charles's illegitimate son with his mistress Barbara Villiers. Twenty years her husband's junior, she was far more restrained than he but was none the less strong-willed, resourceful and ambitious.

In 1866, two years after her husband's death, Blanche Maynard remarried. Her new husband, Lord Rosslyn, was sophisticated, intelligent and, at thirty-three, one of the favourite courtiers of Queen Victoria. He had learned to handle the Queen with both reverence and impudence. (His step-daughter claimed he was the only man in the kingdom who could tell Victoria a risqué joke and get away with it.) In a happy and secure but typically Victorian marriage in which children were seen and not heard, Blanche had a further five children by Rosslyn. In total there were five boys and three girls at Easton Lodge.

A typical upper-class girl, Daisy was educated by nurses, governesses and tutors. Even as an heiress with an enormous income, however, she wore her mother's cast-off dresses. As she grew up she became increasingly like her father in temperament. She was impulsive and quite happy to live dangerously. Francis Greville, Lord Brooke, and later 5th Earl of Warwick, asked to marry Daisy when he was twenty-three and she sixteen. Rosslyn and his wife had hoped to marry her to Prince Leopold of the Belgians, after Benjamin Disraeli, a friend of Rosslyn, had drawn her to the attention of Queen Victoria. They asked Brooke to say nothing to her until Daisy was eighteen, to which he agreed.

In the meantime an inspection of Daisy by the Queen took place at a small, intimate, sombre and unnerving dinner at Windsor Castle. Approval was forthcoming, but Prince Leopold confided to Daisy that he loved someone else and that his friend Lord Brooke had told him of his own love for her. The Prince suggested that she turn him down. When she did so, Brooke proposed next day and Daisy accepted.

Her parents became resigned reasonably quickly, but the Queen was furious. Later she relented and in 1881 asked the newly-weds to dine at Windsor during their honeymoon, commanding the bride to wear her wedding-gown. Victoria later remarked that Daisy's behaviour was 'fast; very fast' when she cut short her stay at Windsor by leaving before breakfast, dressed in her hunting pinks, to attend a meet of the Essex Hunt.

Daisy was an acute observer. She once commented, 'I used to wonder, even as a child, how God viewed this table of precedence [the strict segregation of the upper and lower classes, followed by the strict order of exit] in His church where all men were supposed to be equal.'

In her teens she was sketched by Frank Miles, whose portrait of Lillie Langtry had sold so well. When she was attending one of the final sittings, she and her stepfather met Lillie at the studio. Rosslyn invited the Langtrys to dinner the following evening and then frequently to Easton Lodge, and Lillie became the object of teenage infatuation by Daisy and her sisters.

By the time of her marriage, at which Prince Edward was best man, Daisy had become a considerable beauty and the subject of much male attention, which she did little to discourage. She had also developed a flair for histrionics and a taste for jingoism.

Having come into her inheritance on her marriage, Daisy and her husband now proceeded to enjoy the social benefits of her wealth. There were balls, receptions, dinners, race meetings, Cowes Week, hunting and shooting parties and holidays in the South of France – all activities beloved of Prince Edward. In the first four years of her marriage Daisy gave birth to three children, but soon afterwards she became almost feverishly unfaithful with one of the great adulterers of the period, Lord Charles Beresford. A naval commander, married to a woman much older than himself who made vain attempts to project a youthful image with paint and powder, wigs and other artifices, Beresford was a close friend of Prince Edward. Charles and Daisy became lovers in 1886, and so besotted was she with him that at one point, while the Beresfords were staying at Easton Lodge, she marched into Lady Beresford's room and announced that she was ready to elope with her guest's husband. She was willing to abandon her children and publicly disgrace her husband, herself and her lover.

Lady Beresford took her husband home forthwith, and shortly afterwards it became known that she was pregnant. Since her morals were above
reproach, the child was evidently her husband's, and Daisy became enraged,
even though she herself had had several other liaisons during her infatuation with Beresford. Without pausing to consider that it was not entirely
unexpected that her lover had been in sexual contact with his wife, she wrote
him a nasty and intemperate letter, which was opened by Lady Beresford.

In the ensuing unpleasantness, Daisy enlisted the help of Beresford's
friend Prince Edward to retrieve the letter. This she accomplished after
Edward behaved badly towards both Lady Beresford and his old friend by
falling in love with Daisy himself. It was the start of a nine-year-affair, with
Daisy succeeding Lillie Langtry and Sarah Bernhardt in the Prince's affections. She became the recipient of sentimental rambling letters – often as
many as three a week – in which Edward addressed her as 'Darling Daisy
wife'. He even gave her a ring, a plain gold band which he had been given by
his parents in 1860 and at the same time an ankle bracelet inscribed 'Heav-
ens Above'. They spent time together in Paris; he as Baron Renfrew at the
Hotel Bristol, she under her own name at the Hotel Vendôme nearby. But
Queen Victoria's reach was long, and Edward did not dare attend any Sunday race meetings. Adulterous relationships were one thing; transgressing
his mother's wishes about the day of rest was another.

Daisy was one of the great beauties of her time. It was the ambition of
every man who knew her to be around to pick her up should she fall – 'Upsy
Daisy' – and to comfort her. It was unlikely that Daisy saw herself as a fallen
woman, but according to the mores of the time she was. She was also the
inspiration for the music-hall song 'Daisy Bell':

> Daisy, Daisy, give me your answer do.
> I'm half crazy, all for the love of you!
> It won't be a stylish marriage,
> I can't afford a carriage,
> But you'll look sweet
> Upon the seat
> Of a bicycle made for two!

Lord Brooke's attitude to his wife's affair with the Prince of Wales was remarkably accommodating. In common with many of the men of his set, he sought lovers himself. One lady guest to Easton, having been asked by Lord Brooke to look at the rose garden, found herself enveloped in his arms and told she was by far the most beautiful rose present. Disentangling herself, she rushed to tell her husband about the outrageous behaviour. 'Did he, by Jove!' was the reply. 'Good old Brookie!'

Entertaining on the lavish scale expected by the Prince could be afforded only by a few, and Daisy's wealth ensured that she was one of them. Others nearly ruined themselves in the pursuit of such activity, and it was in such a context that there developed one of the most serious scandals of Edward's life, the Tranby Croft affair, which gave Daisy her nickname of 'Babbling Brooke'. An attempt to hush-up a serious episode of cheating at baccarat during a weekend spent at a country house called Tranby Croft, near Hull, was thwarted when Edward told Daisy about it. Though she subsequently denied it, she is then supposed to have passed on the story at her stepfather's funeral. The pact of secrecy having been broken, the 'guilty' party, Sir William Gordon-Cumming, instructed his solicitors to issue a writ for defamation against his accusers, who included the Prince of Wales. Edward's performance in court in June 1891 was poor, and public opinion sided with Gordon-Cumming even though the jury found against him. Edward was booed by the crowds at Ascot, and his behaviour was the subject of much adverse newspaper comment. The *Review of Reviews* even went so far as to condemn him as 'a wastrel and a whoremonger'.

No sooner was the Tranby Croft affair over than the Beresford con-tretemps was rekindled. Beresford wrote to his wife declaring the Prince of Wales to be 'a blackguard and a coward' in his conduct over the letter that had caused the whole problem. He suggested that Lady Beresford pass it on to Lord Salisbury, the Prime Minister. Frightened by its potential political effect, Salisbury, wrote conciliatory letters to the Beresfords in the hope that they would be a substitute for the public apology they wanted from the Prince.

This did not suffice, and with the publication of a pamphlet by Lady Beresford's sister, Mrs Gerald Paget, a further scandal ensued. Princess

A burnt-out case?
Henry VIII
Line engraving by Peter Isselberg, date unknown

REGIN · THER · EIVS ·   Ā · KĀ · ĪĪĀ · VXOR ·

Paradise lost
Catherine of Aragon, *c.* 1525
Painting attributed to Lucas Horenbout
National Portrait Gallery Picture Library

Paradise regained
Anne Boleyn
Unknown artist and date
National Portrait Gallery Picture Library

'What! All my pretty ones?'
Called Catherine Howard
After Hans Holbein the Younger, no date
National Portrait Gallery Picture Library

A roving eye
Charles II, 1648
Miniature by David Des Granges
National Portrait Gallery Picture Library

An eye to the main chance
Barbara Palmer (*née* Villiers), Duchess of Cleveland, mistress of Charles II, 1666
Artist unknown

National Portrait Gallery Picture Library

'I am the Protestant Whore'
Nell Gwyn, mistress of Charles II, *c.* 1670–5
Portrait by Simon Verelst
National Portrait Gallery Picture Library

Peeping Tom
Samuel Pepys, *c.* 1690–1700
Painting by John Closterman

National Portrait Gallery Picture Library

'Little Pickle'
Actress Dorothy Jordan, mistress of William IV, in the role of the Country Girl
Study by John Ogbourne after George Romney, no date

National Portrait Gallery Picture Library

Flower of her time
The actress Lillie Langtry, mistress of Edward VII, 1885
Photograph by Henry van der Weyde
National Portrait Gallery Picture Library

'My own adored little Daisy Wife'
Frances Evelyn Greville, Countess of Warwick, mistress of Edward VII, 1898
Photograph by Lafayette
National Portrait Gallery Picture Library

Out of court
Mrs Frieda Dudley Ward, mistress of Edward VIII,
with politician Sir Philip Sassoon at Wimbledon, 1922
© *Hulton Getty*

'The Divine Sarah'
French stage actress Sarah Bernhardt, mistress of Edward VII, 1908
Photograph by Marceau
© *Hulton Getty*

Happy and glorious?
Thelma, Lady Furness (left), mistress of Edward VIII, and her twin sister Gloria Vanderbilt
arriving at Southampton on board a cruise liner from the United States, 1935
© *Hulton Getty*

The end of the rainbow
The Duchess of Windsor, formerly Wallis Simpson, 1943
National Portrait Gallery Picture Library

Odds on . . .

Press Association

. . . favourite

Camilla Parker Bowles

Press Association

Alexandra now became embarrassed, and Brooke threatened a divorce action against his wife. This did not materialize, and by the end of 1891 the Beresford scandal fizzled out. However, the deep dislike that Alexandra felt for Daisy was intensified. She had been tolerant of the deferential Lillie Langtry, but would not receive the company of the more assured Lady Brooke. (Alexandra herself had a strictly platonic love-affair with Oliver Montagu, a dashing Blues officer and the younger son of the Earl of Sandwich. He never married, and on his death twenty-five years later she retired weeping to her bed for three days.) Despite the problems that the two scandals had caused, the Prince of Wales's affection for Daisy Warwick remained undiminished. No reconciliation was effected between him and Beresford until 1897.

During the depression of the 1890s Daisy, a practical philanthropist, arranged employment for the local women of Easton by founding a needlework school, whose products were sold in a shop in Bond Street. In 1894 she stood for election as trustee of a local workhouse on a modestly reformist platform. Her influence on Edward was held to be benign, both by his private secretary, Sir Francis Knollys, and by Lady Henry Somerset, president of the British Women's Temperance Association. Daisy disapproved strongly of both heavy drinking and gambling, and her association with W.T. Stead, the leading exponent of campaigning journalism, also contributed to the Prince of Wales's development of a social conscience. Her own Damascene conversion had occurred after a 400-guest ball to mark the end of mourning for her husband's father at Warwick Castle, when a newspaper castigated her for her extravagance.

By 1897 Edward appears to have been finding sexual satisfaction elsewhere and the relationship with Daisy was on the wane. Her developing 'socialist' activities began to take up so much of her time that the Prince's needs could not always be immediately accommodated. She herself had never been in love with the Prince but had craved the influence that her association with him brought.

The affair ended in 1898, when Daisy wrote two letters, one to Alexandra and one to Edward, explaining that the relationship was over. Two months later she discovered, at the age of thirty-six, that she was again pregnant, though probably not with Edward's child. When her son was born she gave him her maiden name of Maynard and never saw the Prince again.

In early 1898, almost at the same time that the relationship with Daisy Warwick ended, Prince Edward met his final and longest-lasting mistress, Alice Keppel, and he was also introduced to Agnes Keyser. Agnes's father was one of the inner circle of financial advisers and bankers who were depended upon by Edward to shore up his fortunes in the face of his huge gambling losses both on the horses and at casinos in France – the financial securities provided by these powerful friends being mistaken for emotional security by the Prince.

Agnes Keyser was well into her forties when she became Edward's confidante and close companion. There is little to suggest that their love-affair was anything other than platonic, apart from Edward's sexual history. Perhaps unwilling to be seen as a rival to the high-profile Alice Keppel, whose relationship with Edward ran in parallel with hers, Agnes would not allow public acknowledgement of the relationship, though, like Alice, she remained by his side for the twelve years until his death. Edward would have known her family not only because her father was one of his financial advisers but also through the Prince's links with other prominent Anglo-Jewish families who were members of his court, such as the Sassoons, the Rothschilds and the Cassels. Sir Ernest Cassel, well ahead of his time, founded the only hospital dedicated to the treatment of mental illness by psychoanalysis, the Cassel Hospital in Richmond, and Siegfried Sassoon, great-nephew of Edward's friend Reuben Sassoon, was intensely involved in social issues. Another member of the circle was Sir Julius Wernher, a South African mining magnate, a generous philanthropist and owner of Luton Hoo, a vast country estate in Bedfordshire.

Agnes was born in 1852. Her family lived at Warren House in Stanmore, Middlesex, and she was the youngest of five children, four of whom were girls. Her mother, Margaret, was the daughter of the architect Edward Blore, and her father, Charles Keyser, was a stockbroker (of Keyser and Ricardo, later Keyser Ullmann) and a great-nephew of David Ricardo of the Dutch Jewish family originally bankers to William of Orange. Little is known of her childhood except that she appears to have been surrounded by women and, according to her great-niece, Anita Leslie, 'ached for the attention of young men' by the time she entered her teens, when she was small, blonde and pretty.

Agnes never married. There were over 600,000 more females than males in the population at the time of her birth, and her independent views on the respective positions of men and women in society tended to make men overlook her in favour of more deferential companions. But Anita Leslie recalls that she adored men and their company and would therefore not have been displeased by Edward's attentions. The family wealth enabled Agnes's brother, Charles, both to pursue unpaid charitable and philanthropic work and to support his four sisters throughout their lives. The family had an ethic of good works, and Agnes dedicated her father's inheritance to charitable causes, particularly in the medical field. She had no need to make herself wealthy through her links with the Prince. She was already extremely rich and cared little for society.

As a young woman, Agnes was restless, irritated by the restrictions of her class and sex, and bored by the conventional social round. At a time when demureness was expected of women and especially of girls, she was bossy and bold when addressing men. When she came up against the Prince of Wales, far from being afraid of him, as were most of his acquaintances, she ordered him about as if he were a small boy. She slipped easily into the (school)mistress role, sensing that Edward – now in his late fifties and obese – was reverting to his childhood and needed taking care of. Whether her relationship with him was sexual is a matter for speculation. It was probably not. As the baby of the family her attachment to her father, who had died six years previously, may well have kept her faithful to his memory.

Having, as a child, had no one to love him but himself, Edward had always found satisfaction in women who, like him, craved attention – mirror images of himself. Playing with them was as gratifying as playing with himself. Only when he was too old for sexual games did he find a woman who genuinely loved him: not Alice Keppel, the long-term mistress who was merely empowered by him, but an unmarried 'Jewish mother', Agnes Keyser, who cooked for him, made a home for him and bestowed tender loving care on him in his later years.

At the outbreak of the second Boer War in 1899, both Agnes and her sister Fanny were encouraged by Prince Edward to help the war effort by pursuing their and his interests in nursing. Edward was a strong supporter of hospitals. He had become patron of eight of them in 1863, the year of his marriage, alone. The two sisters immediately established a nursing-home for sick and wounded officers at 17 Grosvenor Crescent, one of their London homes. (Other ranks were nursed elsewhere, as efficiently but certainly in less luxury, and probably would not have expected otherwise until after the Second World War.) The War Office officially recognized Grosvenor Crescent as a hospital, and 275 officers were nursed there during the three years of the conflict. Fanny Keyser went to South Africa from November 1900 to February 1901 to join a civilian hospital, and her brother founded a home for convalescent soldiers at Aldermaston in Berkshire.

Since, like her sister, Agnes was entirely without nursing training, she confined herself to the running of the Grosvenor Crescent hospital and became its first matron. She showed herself to be an able administrator and persuaded eminent physicians and surgeons to donate their services. Her own staff were employed as domestic servants for the officers. At the end of the war, Edward – now King Edward VII – insisted that the hospital should carry on its work, and under his patronage it became the King Edward VII Hospital for Officers.

Agnes became concerned about her ability to continue to run the hospital out of family funds, so she and King Edward constructed a list of subscribers who would ensure the hospital's future existence, and in 1904 it moved into new, freshly equipped premises at 9 Grosvenor Gardens, which were opened by Edward on 23 April. Agnes – now Sister Agnes – continued to take an active interest in the hospital until her death in 1941. In 1949 the hospital moved to its present site in Beaumont Street, where it was opened by Queen Mary. It is still referred to as Sister Agnes's.

Though Agnes was not liked by Mrs Keppel, who saw her as a rival for Edward's affections, she was an able bridge player and often joined Alice and Edward in a game of cards. Only four days before his death, when he was severely unwell with a chest infection, Edward chose to visit Agnes in preference to seeing Alice. As on many previous occasions when court life bored him, he went to her house in Grosvenor Crescent for the simple meal of Irish stew and rice pudding which she would prepare for him and which he preferred to the rich food he was beginning to find increasingly indigestible. At the very least he enjoyed with Agnes Keyser the pleasures of the nursery: simple food, an understanding and sympathetic listener and the comfort of being told what to do.

Mrs Alice Keppel was arguably the favourite and certainly the longest-running mistress of the Prince of Wales. Twenty-four years younger than his wife, Princess Alexandra, she was born on 29 April 1868, the ninth and last child of Admiral Sir William Edmonstone and Mary Elizabeth Parsons. Alice's father had, more than forty years earlier, been severely wounded in action against pirates off the coast of Crete and had lost part of his lower jaw in the fighting. He was sixty when Alice was born, and his facial disfigurement meant he was no Adonis. Alice adored him, however, and of all his children it was she, the most devoted, who kept vigil at his bedside throughout the last days of his life. Twenty-one years later she repeated the process at the bedside of another not overly attractive father figure, King Edward VII. When he breathed his last, his wife looked tactfully out of the window while his long-time mistress bade him farewell.

Though two years his junior, Alice Keppel mothered her youngest brother, Archie, whom she dominated. Archie was a sensitive, artistic, anxious and vulnerable child who in his teens much preferred gardening to 'manly' pursuits. Alice shared this interest and protected him from the other members of the family. Archie was Alice's doll, the precursor of her daughter Sonia, who would one day truly satisfy her maternal needs. In *Edwardian Daughters* Sonia described Alice's and Archie's mutual affection as 'having the beauty of a theme in a Greek legend . . . a white flame of . . . love for each other'. The two of them shared a nursery in their early childhood, and Alice was apparently devastated when her brother left for further education at the age of thirteen.

Alice was a tomboy. She was keen to play cricket with the staff of her parents' estate and was resentful of privileges given to her male siblings simply because they were boys. She was regarded by her mother as wilful and wild and, though not quick to anger or spiteful, she would throughout her life express her rage physically if sufficiently roused. For example, she boxed the ears of a doctor who set the broken collarbone of her daughter without appropriate gentleness.

Later, when she was developing into a highly attractive woman, she was much sought after at society dinners and weekend parties, at which the customary semi-drunken male flirtatiousness appealed to her. Sonia Keppel recalled how in later life her mother would 'take several moments to raise her veil in male company so that a watching gentleman would catch his breath a little as he beheld her beautiful face'. According to her daughter:

> She had . . . one weakness: she could not allow anyone to be better informed than herself. Whether it was politics, finance or merely the affairs of her friends, the last word, the eventual bombshell of information, must proceed from her and no other. On the whole she preferred her information to be good; and though she was quite prepared to invent what she could not ascertain, she would first make an assault on the main and most reliable source of knowledge.

At the age of twenty-two Alice decided it was time to marry. Her choice of husband was the heavily moustached the Honourable George Keppel, a lieutenant in the Gordon Highlanders. Six foot four inches tall — almost eight foot wearing his busby — he was a striking figure of a man, and Alice thought that he would do.

Alice's father's initially modest circumstances as a naval captain had later improved greatly when he took over the family estates and began selling land off to the railway companies, and the couple were endowed with £20,000 by her family on their marriage. Alice — who was a big spender even by the standards of the time — believed that the Keppels were wealthy and that George shared that wealth. In fact, however, he was substantially less well off than the Edmonstones. His army pay was very little and, apart from a small allowance from his father, the 7th Earl of Albermarle, there was nothing else in the kitty. Most of the once wealthy family's assets had been gambled away by the dowager wife of the 4th Earl.

But it was George Keppel's pedigree that ensured the couple's social position, rather than Alice's family's wealth. She was introduced to the royal court through her husband's uncle, Lieutenant Colonel F.C. Keppel, who was Prince Edward's equerry. And George's great-uncle, Admiral Sir Henry Keppel, was both a former groom-in-waiting to Queen Victoria and an intimate of the Prince of Wales. Admiral Keppel had been involved in a sexual scandal involving the wife of the governor of New Zealand, Sir George Grey – himself a notorious womanizer. That the Admiral survived the scandal was the first proof that sexual promiscuity did not necessarily mean the end of a public career in mid-Victorian England. Had Alice's husband been gifted with foresight he might have ignored her request for an introduction to the court. He was such a loyal monarchist, however, that he did not mind later being known as 'the man who laid down his wife for the King'.

Alice apparently took readily to the extravagance of court society. But, despite George Keppel's pedigree, which had opened doors in society which would otherwise have been closed to her, she came to find her husband not only unattractive but also humourless and sexually cold. George had a kindly nature, but he was intellectually her inferior and had the dubious reputation of being considered 'one of the boys' by his army friends. And when she found out that his once wealthy family was wealthy no more she realized that she had made a mistake. She let it be known to her friends, and probably later to Edward, that she found him sexually inadequate, whereas she was warm, vivacious and thoroughly enjoyed sex. The stuffy formality of the family's ancestral home in Norfolk also contributed to Alice's decision to seek sexual gratification elsewhere.

In 1893, two years after her marriage, she met Ernest William Beckett, the future 2nd Baron Grimthorpe, whose father the 1st Baron Grimthorpe had designed Big Ben. Ernest was a wealthy banker whose wife had recently died, leaving him to care for their three young children. His home, Batchwood Hall, near St Albans, was an imposing manor house standing in more than a hundred acres of land. (It now survives as the impressive club house of an eighteen-hole golf course.) Ernest Becket satisfied two of Alice's desiderata: he not only had money but looked as though he had. He was also a father three times over, and Alice was so enamoured of fathers that within a year of their meeting she was delivered of her daughter Violet. A beautiful baby, Violet was ostensibly George's child, but most of Alice's friends – and enemies – thought she looked very much like Becket. When grown up, as Violet Trefusis she had a stormy love-affair with Vita Sackville-West – causing even more consternation in society than had her notorious mother.

Humphrey Napier Sturt, the 2nd Baron Alington, was next in the queue for Alice's affections, and by now she was developing a sense of social justice. Her daughter Violet recounts coveting a doll in a toyshop window at the time of the Diamond Jubilee in 1897, when Alice was rebelling slightly at the strictures of society. A poor, raggedly dressed child was also eyeing the doll. Alice went inside and bought the doll, then gave it to the poor child, saying to Violet, 'I think she needed it more than you did.'

Alice shamed Sturt into improving his holdings of slum dwellings in Hoxton, one of the poorest areas of London, by asking him to take her there on a carriage drive and expressing her wish that what she saw would be improved in the future. She probably also had a merely platonic relationship with Sir Ernest Cassel, whose advice on the disposition of her initially limited investments made her very wealthy.

In early 1898 Alice was introduced to the 57-year-old Prince of Wales by Baroness Agnes de Stockael at a private lunch. Edward had first seen her while inspecting the Norfolk Yeomanry, in which George Keppel was now an officer, and he was again struck by her beauty. A few weeks later, on 27 February, the 29-year-old Alice and her husband entertained Prince Edward to dinner for the first time. There was an instant meeting of minds, and a rapport arose between Alice and the Prince which continued for the rest of his life.

The liaisons initially took place at the Keppels' Belgravia home at 7 West Halkin Street, while George was spending his days at the St James's Club, having been accepted as a member, after two years of waiting, following intervention by Sir Francis Knollys, the Prince's private secretary and chief procurer. Later meetings took place at Marlborough House, where the Prince of Wales had a suspended harness with footholds that aided copulation, which was otherwise made difficult by his portliness. In time the arrangement became more open, and Alice would stay with the Prince for a 'country-house weekend', an institution that he invented to amuse himself.

To avoid embarrassment, separate invitations to stay at Sandringham would be sent to Alice and her husband, so that George might find himself otherwise engaged without his wife being kept away too.

In *The Glitter and the Gold*, Consuelo Vanderbilt Balsan, who married the Duke of Marlborough in 1895, describes Alice thus:

> Alice Keppel had a short generously-proportioned figure, with small hands and feet, of which she was very proud. When she got older she ran to stoutness and was a perfect match for her portly royal lover. Once when Queen Alexandra saw them together squeezed into a carriage she shook with laughter, calling a Lady-In-Waiting to share the joke. Alice Keppel's head was large and set upon broad shoulders. Her luxuriant chestnut hair was worn in high arrangements. Lustrous blue-green eyes were set off attractively by her alabaster skin. Her lips were full and her deep throaty voice suggested sensuousness . . . In time she was to exhibit the most important qualification of a mistress – she was a good listener.

This last quality was likely to be the major reason why Alice remained in favour with Edward until his death.

Alice Keppel was a competent bridge player, and soothed the sulkiness of Edward when he lost at cards. She once excused herself from his reprimands over a fluffed hand by claiming that she 'could not tell a knave from a king'. She also willingly accommodated his wishes over matters of dress. He insisted upon impeccable style and suitable attire for formal occasions – a matter on which he and his wife did not see eye to eye – though in other respects he could be more relaxed, provided etiquette was observed.

In May 1899 Alice went to Cannes with the Prince for the first time, and later that year it became obvious that she was again pregnant, this time with Sonia. After separate bedrooms had been arranged for the Keppels at their new house at 30 Portman Square, it is highly probable that sexual relations between them had ceased.

After Edward's accession to the throne on the death of his mother in January 1901 his relationship with Alice was conducted openly, and in the

October after Queen Victoria's death she was invited to the Gillies Ball at Balmoral. When Edward rode along London streets, the crowds would call out 'Where's Alice?' and his two-month holiday trips to Biarritz became known among court advisers as 'Mrs Keppel trips'.

That same year Thomas Johnstone Lipton – founder of the Lipton's tea and grocery company, owner of vast tea plantations in Ceylon (Sri Lanka), an ardent socialite and one of Alice's admirers – gave employment to George Keppel in Lipton's vast Buyers Association, which sold everything from groceries to motor cars. This secured the foundation of the couple's income, a continual source of anxiety for Alice, given the demands on her purse of being the mistress of the King.

As Queen Alexandra became more caught up in domesticity, Alice became a link between the King and foreign diplomats and domestic politicians. In 1907, at a dinner at the house of her former lover Humphrey Napier Sturt at Crichel Down in Dorset, after a day's shooting and in the absence of the King, she was seated next to Kaiser Wilhelm. She used the charms that had captivated the King, and, despite his publicly expressed distaste at his uncle Edward's behaviour – though his Prussian aggressiveness and his hostility to women were much more disagreeable – the Kaiser and Mrs Keppel got on well. She saw herself as an unofficial diplomat appointed by the King not only to ameliorate German hostility to Britain but also to improve the increasingly estranged relationship developing between the King and his troublesome nephew. She had done her best to encourage the King to extend the hand of friendship, but the Kaiser had angered Edward more than once in the 1890s. He had particularly given offence during Cowes Week, by treating the occasion not as a sporting and social event but as a symbolic display of the might of the German Navy. Edward did not have the resources to build a more powerful version of his yacht *Britannia* to challenge the Kaiser's huge *Meteor II*, and in 1897 he reluctantly gave up a sport that had given him so much pleasure.

Count Mensdorff, the Austro-Hungarian ambassador, was similarly able to use Alice as a channel through which to pass his personal opinions to Edward while he was being 'punished' by being excluded by the King for his government's behaviour during the Balkan crisis of 1908. Bosnia and Hercegovina had been administered by Austria since the 1878 Treaty of Berlin but had remained under Turkish suzerainty until 6 October 1908, when, without warning, Austria-Hungary arbitrarily breached the agreement and annexed the territory, thus risking war with Russia.

Her growing interest in social conditions also made Alice a conduit through which the opinions of liberal politicians could be put to the King, though the high Tories – under first the Marquess of Salisbury and then Arthur Balfour – deprecated her relationship with Edward and criticized her, and him, openly for it.

It was not until the King's death, in May 1910, that the Establishment decisively turned its back on the King's mistress. Though the Norfolk Yeomanry were represented in the funeral cortège, George Keppel was not invited to take part. The presence of the royal mistress's husband, and possibly also the royal mistress, was too much for the late King's relatives to countenance. At the time of Edward's death Alice's behaviour was hysterical and melodramatic, in marked contrast to the dignity of the Queen. Later, however, she was allowed to attend the final farewell in Westminster Hall, where she conducted herself with due decorum.

On her own death, in 1947, Alice Keppel's estate was found to contain many gifts and mementoes given by her lovers and admirers. Among the most striking was a diamond-and-enamel brooch in the form of four nautical signal flags, a present from Edward. The message spelled out by the flags was 'Position quarterly and open. I am about to fire a Whitehead torpedo straight ahead.'

— 6 —

Edward VIII

The Merry Wives of Windsor

King Edward VIII probably spent most of his adult life looking for the emotional security he lacked as a child. His mother, Princess May of Teck – later Queen Mary – loved him as far as her personality would allow her to, but she had difficulty in showing her feelings towards him. His father, the immature Duke of York, later King George V, had no difficulty whatever in expressing his feelings, both verbally and physically, but he was exceedingly bad-tempered, and his relationship with his son was more aggressive than loving. Edward responded by punishing other men for his father's behaviour towards him, by stealing their women.

The upbringing of Edward VIII and that of his grandfather Edward VII, the relative he most admired, were similar apart from one essential difference: Edward VII was contemptuously devalued by his mother, Queen Victoria, and barely tolerated by his morose father, Prince Albert, whereas Edward VIII had mainly his father to blame for the deficiencies of his childhood.

Prince George – later George V – and his older brother, Albert, the later Duke of Clarence (known to the family as Eddy), were born within eighteen months of one another in 1864 and 1865 and were educated together at the family home of Sandringham. They were brought up almost singlehandedly by their overprotective and smothering mother, Princess Alexandra, with the assistance of a tutor, Mr Dalton, and their only intermittently available father, Edward, Prince of Wales – the future Edward VII. When they were about twelve and thirteen years old, with little or no warning of the abrupt change to their lives, the boys were sent first to Osborne Royal Naval College and later to Dartmouth Naval College, 'to be made men of'.

At first, in an act of thoughtless cruelty, it had been planned that the two brothers – inseparable as children and emotionally dependent on each other as adolescents – would be split up by sending them to different boarding-schools. Their parents soon realized, however, that Eddy, who was virtually ineducable, would not be able to cope on his own at school, so it was decided that the brothers should spend their adolescence away from home in the Royal Navy. George could train for a life at sea, and his older brother could mark time while he waited to inherit the throne. After eight years spent almost entirely in the company of their male fellow cadets and midshipmen, other than when on shore leave, they emerged bewildered and confused about what was expected of them.

'Eddy' attracted considerable scandal in his early twenties. With his friend Lord Euston, he was discovered by the police in a central-London homosexual brothel, and shortly afterwards he achieved still greater notoriety; he was briefly one of the suspects in the investigations of the murderer later known as Jack the Ripper, after the body of the first prostitute victim was found in Whitechapel in the early hours of the morning of 31 August 1888. Claims have even been made that Eddy did not in fact die at his home in Sandringham a few days after his twenty-eighth birthday in 1892, despite being reported as having done so by his family. The story goes that he died years later, in 1933, having been incarcerated in Glamis Castle following his marriage to a Catholic commoner, Annie Crook, in about 1885. He is also said to have fathered her child, Alice, who died in 1950. Glamis Castle has been shown to have one more room than it has windows, and supporters of this conspiracy theory believe that the windowless room was Eddy's prison. Such theorists also claim that the Ripper murders were the work of a group authorized by high authority to protect the reputation of the presumably bisexual Duke from threats of blackmail by prostitutes who had been his sexual partners.

Before his death a marriage had been arranged for the Duke, and the candidate chosen was Princess May of Teck, a member of the relatively poor German branch of Queen Victoria's extended family. Growing up in a milieu of immense wealth that would never be hers unless she married into it, the Princess was persuaded by her mother, Princess Adelaide, Queen Victoria's obese and avaricious German cousin, to accept Eddy's offer of marriage. She was not pleased by her mother's choice, but as time passed she grew to accept her fate, taking the view that to be Queen of England was more than adequate compensation for marriage to an unintelligent male of doubtful sexual orientation. In fact Princess May was devastated when her fiancé died. She had grown fond of him, and had come to admire qualities of kindliness and concern which at first had not been apparent.

His younger, shy, self-conscious and immature brother George, now heir to the throne, was meanwhile waiting in the wings hoping that no one would notice him. George had grown up confused by the dichotomy between the smothering love which his mother had directed towards him as a young child and the apparent withdrawal of her love when he had been banished from home for the entire period of his adolescence. The Navy might have made a man of him, but it was before he was ready to stop being a boy. Reluctant to grow up, as an adult he collected mechanical toys, stamps and pictures of young children. George adored children, though he was unable to cope with intimacy. He had gone from early childhood to adulthood with little time between the two, and for much of his life he remained a child, albeit in man's clothing, the child whom his mother had once loved.

When he was thirteen George had fallen in love with Julia Stonor, also thirteen, whose mother was one of Princess Alexandra's ladies-in-waiting. Their 'romance' continued throughout his life, even after her marriage to the Catholic Marquis d'Hautpoul. The 'child' in George related to the 'child' in Julia, and they exchanged letters until his death.

George had no other experience of women apart from a crush on his thirteen-year-old cousin who would later become Queen Marie of Romania. He now found himself being put forward as a replacement for his much-loved older brother, not only as heir to the throne but as a fiancé for the grieving Princess May. Their marriage arose not so much out of love as out of a sense of duty by Prince George and out of Princess May's conviction that it was her destiny to be Queen of England and to help restore her parents' fortunes.

On 6 July 1893, in the presence of the depressed Queen Victoria and other crowned heads of Europe in the Chapel Royal at St James's Palace, the

Archbishop of Canterbury married Princess May to Prince George, Duke of York. Seventeen years later, following the death of King Edward VII, their coronation took place in the pomp and glory of Westminster Abbey, and the former Princess finally took the title of Queen Mary.

The Duchess of York gave birth to her first child, Edward, on 23 June 1894. His 29-year-old father wrote in his diary on that day that at '10.00 a sweet little boy was born'. But as Edward grew older his father's initial sentimentality changed to 'chaffing' – often a synonym not so much for friendly teasing as for demeaning ridicule.

Neither of Edward's parents had much idea of how to bring up children, though his upbringing was clearly influenced by the effect of the Navy on his father. As a child, the Duke of York had been bullied by his fellow cadets at Naval College, and he became a timid, self-conscious man who expressed his anger by shooting, in the name of sport, vast numbers of animals and by frightening his children with his outbursts of uncontrolled rage, supposedly in the interests of discipline. Though some of his supporters have dismissed this as apocryphal, it seems that he would terrify his children and anyone else within earshot by repeatedly impressing them with information that they did not want to hear about his attitude to fathering: 'My father', he would shout, 'was frightened of his mother; I was frightened of my father; and I am damned well going to see to it that my children are frightened of me.'

As his family grew, it became obvious that the Duke could tolerate children only for brief periods. That children should be seen but not heard was the received wisdom among upper-class families. Edward's father believed this to be written in stone and enforced it with unnecessary brutality. So, like most other royal children of the time, Edward saw little of his natural parents. They were largely content to leave their son's early upbringing in the hands of Mary Peters, an abusive nanny whose love for her charge was tainted by a streak of overt cruelty. His nanny, his surrogate parent and the woman to whom he had bonded in the absence of his mother, was so besotted with him that she would pinch him or twist his arm to make him cry before entering the drawing-room at 6 p.m. where her freshly scrubbed charge was due to spend the ritual half-hour with his parents. The Duke of

York, unable to tolerate anything so disruptive as a crying child in his obsessively ordered space, would instruct Peters to take him away again. It was three years before Edward's mother discovered that her son seemed to have permanently bruised arms. The nanny was instantly dismissed and locked away in a mental institution.

Mary Peters later claimed that if she had abused her charge it was only in the interests of her love for him. This may well have been true, but in the process she neglected Edward's brother George, known as 'Bertie', eighteen months his junior, often forgetting to feed him. The below-stairs staff were terrorized by the nanny and did not speak up for the boys. (Many years later Bertie – by now George VI – partially redressed the balance in his favour by ostracizing Edward after his abdication.)

Mary Peters was replaced by the cockney Lala Bill, who soothed, stroked and comforted Edward, though he had to share her with his younger brother.

Little is known of the private life of the Duke and Duchess of York, but their formality and rigidity were probably at the expense of spontaneity and passion. After they had come to the throne, at night they would sit at either end of the long dining-table at Buckingham Palace wearing clothes more appropriate to a state banquet than to a private dinner. If they were as detached from their sexual appetites as they were from their gastronomic ones they would have been poor role models for their children, who would always have imagined them as at arm's length from each other. The Duke was an emotional man, but his emotions took the form of uncontrolled rage, which made his son's childhood a gilded cage from which Edward could not wait to escape.

The Duke insisted that the beatings of *his* childhood had made a man of him. He had no hesitation in applying this principle to his son and heir. Even at the age of eighteen Edward was so frightened of his father that he would faint not only when he shouted at him but even when he was summoned to his study. In his autobiography, *A King's Story*, he describes how the words 'His Royal Highness wishes to see you in the Library' would fill him with terror, for they were usually a prelude to admonition and reproof. According to Philip Ziegler's biography of Edward VIII, the Duke of York loved and wanted the best for his children, but he was a bad-tempered and often frightening man. He was never cruel, but he was a harsh disciplinarian who believed that a bit of bullying never did a child any harm; he shouted, ranted and struck out verbally and physically to express his displeasure. Alec Hardinge, a royal secretary, said, 'It was a mystery why George V, who was such a kind man, was such a brute to his children.'

Today an industry has grown up around the association of physical punishment with sex. Many clients of brothels whose preferences are for 'discipline' are upper-class men whose parents believed that their sons should be beaten 'for their own good'. As children, such sons may have received more attention when they misbehaved than when they were being good. And if the comforting hands of a nanny followed the abuse, the distinction between pain and pleasure was even more likely to become blurred.

The once commonplace beating of male children by a parent or teacher says more about the oppressor than the victim. The statement 'this hurts me more than it hurts you' with which such punishment is often defended is a falsehood. Though the aim of such treatment is to instil in the child respect not only for his elders but for authority, it does not work, and the abused child may grow up to be an abusing parent. The Duke of York was simply passing on to his children the emotional stresses to which he himself had been exposed by his parents and their surrogates.

Just as he always loved the child in Julia Stonor, the Duke also loved the child in his son Edward, but he kept him at arm's length by shouting at him and telling his nanny to keep him away when he cried. The child was probably too close to him for his own peace of mind, and his way of coping with the problem of this overwhelming attachment, from which he suffered throughout his life, was to do to his son what his parents had done to him: make a man of him as quickly as possible, before he had done with being a boy.

With this in mind, at the age of twelve Edward was also enrolled as a naval cadet, and his childhood, like his father's thirty years earlier, came to an abrupt end. 'Then the fateful day of leaving arrived, and my father took me away to Osborne,' he wrote in his memoirs. 'Despite my most determined efforts to uphold what I guessed must be the traditions of the British Navy, I left Marlborough House with tears drenching my new blue uniform.'

Prince Edward's education was similar to that of other children of wellborn families and echoed that of his father. The Duke of York had gone to naval college, and he took the attitude that if it had been good enough for him it would certainly be good enough for his children. It might well have been had Edward been less sensitive and more robust. At first at Osborne and later at Dartmouth he was the victim of bullying by other cadets, who took the opportunity of cruelly teasing a child who apparently did not know his surname. In his autobiography, written years later, he made light of events that today would alert the social services. He describes a mock ceremony in which the window of an empty classroom would be raised enough to push his head through then slammed down on the back of his neck as 'a crude reminder of the sad fate of Charles I and the English method of dealing with Royalty who displeased'.

Edward accepted the bizarre cruelty and bullying of the midshipmen at Osborne as routine. He did not like it but never questioned it. He could not perpetuate the cycle with his own children because he had none. He did, however, retaliate against the Establishment by turning his back on it. He remembered one episode in particular at Osborne, when the cadet captains, who represented the Establishment for the cadets, had devised a vicious 'game':

One evening while we were undressing in our dormitory, the cadet captain rang the bell for silence. He told us that we were a lazy bunch of 'warts' and that we needed a good shake-up. He went on to announce that the time allowed for undressing and putting on our pyjamas before running down to the wash-house would be reduced from one minute to thirty seconds. Though we were used to doing everything at the double and obeying orders unquestioningly, this order was the last straw. The inevitable result was a series of summonses to the wash-house after 'lights-out' and a harsh application of the gong rope to any boy who failed to meet the deadline.

When Edward wrote to his mother explaining as best he could without being too explicit that 'there is an awful rush here, and everything has to be done so quickly', he may have hoped that she would read between the lines and intervene on his behalf. But, in her response she merely reminded him to be sure to leave time to clean his teeth.

By the time Edward was eighteen his formal education was deemed to have ended. What he had gained from his childhood was a sense of servility – later translated into a desire to serve – and an exaggerated respect for his parents. At naval college he had learned very little other than to be even more wary of bullies than he was before he went away. And after two years at Magdalen College, Oxford, he had learned nothing more. But his father thought he would benefit from being given a commission in the Grenadier Guards.

Surprisingly, Edward took to life in the Guards. If he was not in command of himself, he was at least in command of others. He was by now so subdued by authority that the first signs of compensatory risk-taking began to emerge. The bullied Prince had not turned into a bully himself, which was often the outcome of the childhood and education he had endured, but into an often depressed young man in need of excitement to counter his frequent episodes of gloom.

At the outbreak of the First World War, Edward demanded of Lord Kitchener, the Secretary for War, that he be sent to the front, arguing that, if he were killed, there would still be four brothers to ensure the continuity of the monarchy. With a brutal frankness that the Prince would probably not even have noticed, Kitchener told him that he would not be concerned if the Prince were killed, but it would certainly worry him if he were captured. Edward was therefore restricted to staff appointments. It is not certain that Edward particularly wanted to kill Germans. In fact he admired them and had fond memories of his visit to Germany in 1913 to meet the favourite grandson of Queen Victoria, his father's cousin Kaiser Wilhelm. If he were captured, he was sure that his Onkel Willie would look after him. Had he been closer to its horrors, however, the war might well have helped him confront his suppressed feelings and perhaps might even have encouraged him to take more responsibility both for them and for his duty to his country.

It was not long before Edward found an alternative high-risk outlet for his depression. His first sexual experience was probably with Paulette, a prostitute in France who was the regular consort of an officer in the Royal Flying Corps. His equerries Piers 'Joey' Legh and Claud Hamilton introduced her to him, and Edward's revealing diary comment towards the end of 1916 was that she was 'a heavenly little woman of the kind'. She must have helped him overcome his only previous experience of commercial sex, which had involved watching a prostitute striking erotic poses in a brothel in Calais. He had written in his diary that it was 'a perfectly filthy and revolting sight'. He seemed to have been so negatively affected – possibly by the absence of any romantic or at the very least affectionate factor in the brothel scene – that in May 1916, after he had met Paulette, he wrote to his friend Captain W.R. Bailey, a fellow Guards officer, 'I hope that you are home by now and having a jolly good time and are appeasing your sexual hunger, which I more than understand, tho' don't actually experience it myself, strange to say.' The most likely explanation for his indifference to the charms of the brothel and Paulette is that love that was available and unstinting was of little interest to him. He had been brought up to expect love from his parents only when he pleased them. His experiences as a child with Mary Peters, whose need for Edward was so great that she encouraged his parents to curtail the few moments they had with him at the end of each day, ensured that he was more likely be in touch with his loving feelings when being rejected.

After his introduction to Paulette, Edward became more interested in women and resented the time spent on leave at Sandringham, where he crocheted after dinner. 'What an occupation for a fellow on leave! I can't raise much enthusiasm over anything except women!' he wrote in one letter. Queen Mary, who spent most of her leisure time working on vast tapestries, had taught him to sew as a child, and between the ages of eight and thirteen Edward would sit at her feet on a small stool looking up at his mother with adoration. This was a position he was to adopt with most women who entered his life, other than those whom he paid for sex.

In July 1917 he spent his leave in Paris in what his diary referred to as 'three days bliss' with a French woman, Maggy, to whom he wrote love-letters and whom he had almost certainly not looked up to. He had asked her to burn his letters, but, like his grandfather's letters to another prostitute, also in Paris, the documents survived and were recovered later only at some cost.

In London during the early part of the war, and before he had been introduced to commercial sex, Edward fell in love for the first time – with Viscountess Marion Coke. Twelve years older than Edward, Marion lived at Holkham Hall, near the Sandringham estate. Her father-in-law, Lord Leicester, and Edward's father had been shooting companions for years. Small, vivacious and a good dancer, she provided a foil to Edward's depressing home life, where the King's demeanour and inability to communicate with his children deadened the atmosphere.

For ten years Marion had been happily married to Viscount 'Tommy' Coke, heir to the Earl of Leicester, and she knew better than to cross forbidden boundaries. Edward's letters to her from France in 1915 became increasingly desperate when she tried to limit her role to that of confidante and confessor. However, she was undoubtedly flattered by the Prince's protestations of love, and she occasionally encouraged him in his post-adolescent longings. She was mortified when, after writing love-letters to her for three years, he suddenly ended all contact with her.

Edward could change his allegiances from one minute to the next if he felt rejected. It was probable that their relationship was not a sexual one, but they had known one another for some time and Marion had no reason to believe that one day the Prince would cut her dead. But, like all insecure children, Edward had never learned to trust anyone. Either he was loved or he was not, and if he was not he would look elsewhere. Marion Coke's mistake was to call the tune in their relationship. She was the prototype of all the other women with whom Edward was to fall in love. Teasing was unacceptable. He was unable to tolerate any hint of rejection.

Edward's mistresses all appear to have been cast in the same mould. Most were married women and therefore in theory unavailable. As a child he had always fought for love: it had never been given freely. He had therefore to make a conquest. As soon as he had overcome whatever doubts a woman he fell for might have had, he would give her up as abruptly as he had given up Marion and look for other women with whom he could renew the struggle to overcome their reluctance to give him the love he craved. If, as usually happened, he succeeded at least temporarily in gaining the undivided attention of a married woman he would also have satisfied his other need: the rejection of a husband. By sending Edward away to naval college at the age of twelve, his father had stolen his mother – and her love – from him. Many of the women to whom Edward later turned were married, often with children. To steal them from their husbands – the 'fathers' to whom they were married – was to retaliate for his own mother having been stolen from him; and to look on them as surrogate mothers was entirely appropriate to his needs. Getting a rival to be disadvantaged was far better than being rejected himself, and to take a mother away from a father and be the sole recipient of her love had always been his ambition. He was comfortable with Marion because she was like the rest of the Sandringham social circle, not excluding his mother, but he had hoped that she would be his accomplice in depriving her husband of her company. Unaware that this was the role she was expected to play, she kept Edward at what she thought was a socially acceptable arm's length. By doing so she lost him altogether.

At more or less the same time as his passion for Marion Coke, the 21-year-old Edward – still prey to barely controllable adolescent desires – also found himself attracted to Lady Sybil ('Portia') Cadogan. Despite being big and clumsy (albeit an enthusiastic dancer) and not particularly pretty, Portia had a powerful personality, though with less charm and spontaneous gaiety than Marion. One of the five daughters of the Earl of Cadogan, she was a close friend of Edward's younger sister, Princess Mary.

Edward met Portia at Windsor in 1915 and immediately fell in love with her. Their affair, such as it was, lasted for about a year, but – before his sexual initiation with Paulette in France – was unlikely to have been consummated. It is possible that they may have used up much of their passion by exploring the sexual metaphors in golf, their favourite leisure activity. Edward wrote frequent love-letters to her and asked that she burn them, a request with which she showed no hesitation in complying. Lovers are usually reluctant to give up mementoes that remind them of their happy days together, but this time Edward did not read the warning signs correctly.

Perhaps not unexpectedly, their relationship ended abruptly. Without warning, in June 1917, only days after Edward had discussed the possibility of marriage to Portia with his mother – who had assured him that no one would put pressure on him to marry anyone, especially someone he did not love – Portia became engaged to someone else. Her fiancé, whom she later married, was Edward Stanley (son of Lord Derby), one of the Prince's friends from his days at Oxford, and she later married him. Her telegram to her parents announcing her betrothal said simply 'Engaged to Edward', leading them to believe that they were about to become linked to the royal family. Prince Edward was devastated, as was Portia's mother. Left with no one to comfort and reassure him, and with his leave coming to an end, the Prince returned to France to rejoin his regiment.

Earlier, as the future Edward VIII set out to redeem his lost childhood, he had met a princess who might have been a suitable life partner. Just before the First World War, when he was twenty years old, he was staying at Gotha in Germany when he met Caroline Matilda, Princess May of Schleswig-Holstein. Though tall and slim, Princess May was no beauty. She had a red nose and her teeth were poor, but she had a pleasant personality. Years later the older, but not wiser, Edward admitted to his equerry Godfrey Thomas, 'I could have done worse.' Thomas was convinced that, had the war not intervened, the two would have married. And King George V lived to regret that when his son met Caroline Matilda he did not press him to settle down.

On leave in London in February 1918, still sad at the abrupt ending of his relationship with Portia, Edward quite by chance met Mrs Winifred ('Frieda') Dudley Ward during an air raid. Frieda was the wife of William Dudley Ward, who had been the MP for Southampton since 1906 and was now the Liberal whip. Dudley Ward was sixteen years older than his wife and a well-connected aristocrat – the nephew of the 1st Earl of Dudley and the grandson of the 1st Viscount Esher – as well as a Cambridge rowing blue. He was also the vice-chamberlain of the royal household from 1917 to 1922. He and Frieda had married in 1913, but, despite their two children, by the time Frieda met the Prince they were leading largely separate lives.

Frieda was born on 28 July 1894 and so was a few weeks younger than Edward, though she outlived him by eleven years. She grew up in Lamcote,

Radcliffe-on-Trent, Nottinghamshire, and was the elder of two daughters of
Colonel Charles Birkin, a prosperous lace manufacturer, and his American
wife, Claire Howe. She was not close to either of her parents and felt even
more distanced from them after her younger sister Vera was born. In *The
Duchess of Windsor*, Greg King quotes from an unpublished manuscript in
which a friend said of Frieda 'she was absolutely fascinating to look at, she
had a good mind, a tremendous character, great loyalty and wonderful sense
of humour. She built one up and made one feel amusing and attractive. She
had a strong influence on us all.'

Frieda was elegant, petite and pretty, though her most distinctive feature
was her high-pitched, thin and reedy voice. She was considered charming,
tactful and discreet. Sixteen years later, when her affair with the Prince was
over, she conducted herself with dignity, and she made no attempt to capital-
ize on his fall from public favour following his decision to abdicate. 'Be
discreet. Be like Mrs Keppel. Be discreet' was the advice of Reginald Brett,
2nd Viscount Esher, to whom Frieda was related by marriage. And she was.

Though she contrived to appear frail and feminine, she was a good golfer
and tennis player and by no means 'a pretty little fluff', as Cynthia Asquith
called her in her diaries. Her influence on Edward was seen by his staff as
almost entirely for the good. 'One of the best friends he ever had in his life' is
how she was described by Bruce Ogilvy, one of the Prince's equerries. A
chain-smoker herself, she not only managed to encourage Edward to reduce
his consumption of tobacco but also made him eat more, something that his
equerries had failed to achieve.

Their first meeting came about after Frieda was walking across Belgrave
Square with an escort one evening. When an air-raid warning sounded,
Frieda and her companion stood in the doorway of Mrs Maud Kerr-Smiley's
house in the square, where the Prince was the guest of honour at a private dinner party. Maud Kerr-Smiley – the sister of Ernest Simpson, who would later
marry the divorced Wallis Spencer – invited them to shelter in her basement
until the all-clear sounded. Edward took Frieda away from her escort and
spent the remainder of the evening dancing with her, while Zeppelins intermittently flew overhead. Having made what he hoped had been a conquest,
he spent the next sixteen years of his life in an often hopeless battle to retain it.

The day after they met, Edward wrote to Frieda asking if he might visit her. Frieda was staying with her mother-in-law, who opened the letter in the belief that it was for her. She was disappointed to find that it was not. That letter was the first of many. Throughout their relationship Edward wrote to Frieda at least once a day, and often more frequently. In 1996, 263 letters and photographs previously thought to have been lost were discovered in Canada. They had been bought twenty years earlier by a stamp collector who, when he lost interest in stamps, had stored them in a trunk in his attic and more or less forgotten about them. In 1999 they were edited and published by Rupert Godfrey. Their yearning, badly spelled and badly punc-tuated baby-talk style is like that of a child to a mother. Frieda, herself a mother, would not have been immune to his need to be cared for. Her letters to him are missing, and little is known of her true feelings, but it says a great deal for the relationship that their correspondence continued for years and that she never discarded any of his letters. One can only conclude that her interest in her boyish lover suggests that the relationship that suited both of them was that of parent and child, rather than one between adults.It is sig-nificant that, apart from his later wife, Wallis Simpson, who was childless, and whose dominating and controlling personality was closer to Edward's experience of his father, many of the women to whom the Prince was attracted were themselves mothers.

The first of the letters was written in March 1918, while Edward was at GHQ, British Forces in Italy, a few months before the war came to an end; the last dates from January 1921. Many of them were written from HMS *Renown*, when he was separated from Frieda by his official tours of the Empire. All begin with endearments ranging from 'Angel!!!!' to 'Beloved Angel' or 'My own sweet Angel', and usually end with 'tons and tons of love from your devoted E'. Though providing some information about friends and family, they contain essentially the sad and hopeless longings of an unloved child whose passions are emphasized by the distance between him and their recipient. Expressing something like a schoolgirl crush, they are an echo of the arm's-length love of the Prince's childhood, a love intensified through suffering and pain.

The letters not only reveal the nature of Edward's love for Frieda but also demonstrate his need both to reassure her of it and to convince her of the seriousness of his intentions. They are punctuated with adolescent sexual innuendo and throw light on his sexual needs. Kissing is overemphasized (some letters end with *'des milliers des baisers les plus tendres!!!!'*), as is the recounting of what for the time were risqué jokes. In one letter he says, 'I've got another worse one for you, darling, only don't be shocked, but I could not be shy with you and would tell you anything: – (The big gun that shoots at Paris is called Rasputin because it comes once every 15 minutes!!!!).' Edward goes on to ask her to send him any jokes or stories she hears – 'because I love them'. On one occasion, while at sea en route to begin his 1919 Canadian tour, the Prince wrote, 'I shall miss my very own darling beloved little mummie so terribly & all her comfort & advice.'

Though Edward certainly had missed out on mothering, and his emotional dependency on Frieda must have been something of which both were aware, 'mummie' may well have been merely an affectionate diminutive between them. Neither would have been more than dimly aware of the roles they were playing. Edward, immature in height and weight as well as in intellect, retained a boyish charm to the end of his life.

From the start of their relationship, Frieda hung on to all her numerous other male admirers as emotional chaperones. The Prince of Wales – as he had been styled since 1910 – thought of them as his rivals. As a child he had been intensely jealous of his five siblings, assuming that, since he was not the recipient of his parent's love, it must of necessity be going to others more deserving. One man in particular whom he resented was Michael Herbert, the younger brother of the Earl of Pembroke. Herbert – who was very fond of Frieda and jealous of Edward – was frequently referred to in the Princes's letters: on one occasion Edward begged Frieda not to dance with him when they met socially. Another rival was the American socialite and polo player Rodman Wanamaker, whom the Prince contemptuously referred to as 'Pappapacker', and yet another was Major Reginald Seymour, who had been seriously wounded in France and was an equerry to King George. Frieda referred to them all as 'the barrage', hoping that Edward would be reassured by her levity; but he continued to experience them as a constant threat. In September 1923 he wrote, 'Their kind might be all right for an affair but I guess that's about all.'

Edward's tendency to hyperbole – compensation for his understated childhood – never left him. In a letter dated 11 April 1920, fourteen months after meeting Frieda, Edward wrote, ' Now I am going to write something that I know I ought not to really – but mon amour I swear I'll never marry another woman but YOU!!!' But Edward's biographer Philip Ziegler has stated that the intensity of the relationship cooled dramatically after the first eighteen months, with Frieda becoming increasingly brutal in her unsuccessful attempts to cool the Prince's ardour. The Prince responded by swearing undying love and, for good measure, promising to give up the throne for her. Frieda was in many ways very much like Edward. Neither of them had learned to cope with closeness, and they spent their lives avoiding commitment. For many years their various affairs protected them from forming one single relationship. Frieda was unable to cope with the intensity of his longing, and the more he demanded intimacy the more anxious she became. She danced with him but was uneasy about getting into bed with him, metaphorically or otherwise.

By 1922 there was talk of a divorce from her husband, which sent Edward into paroxysms of anxiety. He was touring the Far East at the time and had to rely solely on Frieda's replies to his letters for information. It was a reflection of his fear of intimacy that his most passionate feelings were reserved for women who were unavailable, and he was almost certainly relieved that the divorce story was merely a rumour. Not until 1932 was Frieda divorced from the husband she had deceived for years. The divorce nalled the beginning of the end of her affair with the Prince.

Since nothing was known about Edward's passionate letters to Frieda until 1996 her association with him seemed at the time respectable and above board. Society recognized it as serious but nothing more. That Edward told her he would give up his throne for her was known to no one. Frieda was so discreet that at first even her husband raised no objection to her friendship with the Prince, and Lord Esher found 'nothing objectionable' in it. Edward's staff and friends respected her. But by the end of the 1920s he had found someone who was a more enthusiastic games player.

Frieda and Edward remained friends, however. In 1919 Frieda had chosen the interior furnishings for York House, the Prince's home in a wing of St James's Palace, and in 1930 he asked her to advise on the redecoration of Fort Belvedere, his grace-and-favour home at Sunningdale on land bordering Windsor Great Park. As a young adult she had been much in demand for her views on interior design. Indeed, she made her living by buying houses, renovating them and then selling them. But, though she could make homes for others, she never succeeded in creating an enduring home for herself. Five years after her divorce from William Dudley Ward she married the Marquis de Casa Maury. Her second marriage was dissolved in 1954.

In March 1918 Edward, not yet considering Frieda as a possible candidate for his next mistress, had met Lady Rosemary Leveson-Gower, the daughter of the 4th Duke of Sutherland and niece of the Earl of Rosslyn. He is thought to have considered marrying her but to have been been put off by his mother, who told him there was mental illness in Rosemary's mother's family. Rosemary was killed in a plane crash returning from Le Touquet in 1930. (Piers 'Joey' Legh, Edward's long-time equerry, narrowly avoided the same fate. His wife's fear of flying had led them to return home by sea.)

Then, despite his protestations of undying love for Frieda, during a trip to the USA in 1922 Edward became attracted to Rita Kruger, a woman who bore more than a passing physical resemblance to Wallis Simpson. In 1923 he had a brief affair with Audrey James, who shortly after he met her married Major Dudley Coates. Her husband took a much less compliant view of his wife's behaviour than had William Dudley Ward, and had no hesitation in telling Edward what he thought of him. At the end of that August, Edward wrote to Frieda about a house party where Dudley Coates and Audrey were also guests: 'the air is electric and its all too tricky for words. I'm quite exhausted and shall be lucky if I escape without a hell of a row.' He went on to say, 'I'm *not* madly in love and never will be again and she'll never mean a fraction to me of what you do.' According to a mutual friend, Audrey James was too possessive for Edward's taste. And this was an affair where the husband did not retire hurt, as did others, but fought back.

Edward had to win. But if he lost there were always other women, often on one or other of his many tours abroad. His relationships with them were usually brief flings, the sexual forays of a soldier who, protected by his uniform, takes what he wants from women and then moves on. He would confide in Frieda about these like a child confessing to his mother that he had been naughty. Then, like any other 'good' mother, Frieda would forgive rather than chastize him.

There were many instances when the Prince sought out other naughty children with whom to play. According to Philip Ziegler, on a Nairobi safari in 1928 Gladys Lady Delamere 'bombarded him with pieces of bread, and ended up by rushing at him, overturning his chair and rolling around on the floor with him at the Muthaiga Club', an exclusive rendezvous for upper-class expatriates. Another, equally brief, fling – also in 1928 in Nairobi – was with the wife of an unnamed British official. According to his own account to Alan Lascelles, his private secretary, Edward spent the evening seducing her after receiving news that his father was thought to be dying from the lung abscess so far unsuccessfully treated by incompetent doctors. He was told by Lascelles that he should return home immediately. Edward's equerry resigned after the Nairobi trip, not only in disgust at the Prince's sexual behaviour but because Edward was more concerned with charming women, most of whom queued up to be charmed, than with his father's health.

Apart from Frieda, there was at this time no one to whom the Prince was more attached than the beautiful Thelma, Lady Furness. Thelma had married Marmaduke, the 2nd Lord Furness, in 1926, having divorced James Vail 'Junior' Converse a year earlier. Converse was a well-known playboy 'financier' and had squandered his inheritance from his grandfather, one of the founders of the Bell Telephone Company. Edward's parents respected Frieda Dudley Ward, who was discreet and whose family was well connected and well liked, but they were appalled by his relationship with the divorced and remarried Thelma.

Despite King George's reservations about Thelma's background, he could scarcely have complained of her lack of education – though it was certainly fragmented, albeit no more so than that of many children of diplomats in the foreign service. Indeed he may have envied her it, since his own education had hardly been a success. Thelma was born in 1904 in Lucerne, where for a time her father was American consul. She attended schools and convents in several European countries, including Belgium, England, Germany and Spain, and in the USA. Her later unsettled attitude to life was probably based on the many changes to which she was exposed as a child. Her father, Harry Hays Morgan, was a member of an old Southern family. Her mother, Laura Kilpatrick, another Southerner, claimed to be related to Spanish royalty, though it is likely that Thelma inherited from her mother a background more akin to *Gone with the Wind* than one with roots in Castile.

In his diaries from the late 1920s Cecil Beaton described Thelma and her twin sister, Gloria, as noted beauties, 'as alike as two magnolias and with their marble complexions, raven tresses and flowing dresses, with their slight lisp and foreign accents, [diffusing] an Ouida atmosphere of hothouse elegance and lacy femininity'. The twins' childhood was dominated by the behaviour of their superstitious, domineering and volatile mother. Their father was kindly but remote, content to leave their mother alone in return for a life untroubled by domestic friction. Just before the marriage, Laura Kilpatrick had procured her future husband's appointment abroad by playing the Southern belle and pulling strings with President Harding, and she never let him forget that his advancement in the foreign service was entirely due to her. Her behaviour was alternately vicious and doting. On returning from a trip abroad during which the girls were left in the care of their domestic servants, their mother ordered that their pet pigeons be released and the pigeon chicks be roasted and served to the twins for dinner – because, according to Spanish superstition, pigeons were supposedly bad luck. The servants were so terrified of Mrs Morgan that this act of thoughtless cruelty was reluctantly carried out.

Harry Hays Morgan was loving, but seldom around, and Thelma could not get on with her dominant and aggressive mother. She planned to leave home as soon as she was able.

Thelma's relationship with Junior Converse had begun in elopement. He and Thelma married in 1920 in Maryland, one of the few states to allow females to marry at sixteen. (The reception was held at the Chevy Chase Country Club in New York, where Wallis Simpson's mother worked as a hostess.) The marriage lasted legally until 1925, when she divorced him, though it had effectively been over about two years after it began.

Converse was an alcoholic and a failure at business, and Thelma had to rely on a modest allowance from her father and the help of her twin sister –

now the enormously wealthy Gloria Vanderbilt – for her living expenses. She fled to Paris to get away from her husband and then returned to stay with her sister in California. Her beauty got her bit parts in the movies, where she met the heavy-drinking Richard Bennett, a silent-movie matinée idol, who was the father of two much loved film-stars of the 1930s, Joan and Constance Bennett. Though she was still married to Converse, Bennett gave her a diamond ring and asked her to marry him. After some heart-searching, Thelma turned him down and went once more to stay with her sister. At a dinner party she met the heir to the Furness Withy shipping fortune, the uncouth Marmaduke Furness.

Twenty-one years older than his future wife, Marmaduke – or 'Duke' as Thelma called him – was considered by those close to him to be foul-mouthed and arrogant, but Thelma was totally overwhelmed by him. It was a reflection on her judgement that she regarded him as one of the ablest businessmen in England, whereas his father, the founder of the family business, reluctant to have his assets squandered, had thought so little of his son that he left everything to a distant cousin. But this sensible plan did not work. Not long after Marmaduke's father's death in 1912, the cousin died in a car accident and the fortune reverted to Marmaduke. As the result of what some would say was his undeserved inheritance, he became, according to Thelma, a force in the City of London, where, she claimed, his word was always his bond.

Despite the beauty of his new young wife, Marmaduke had numerous affairs, taking the view – heavily subscribed to in the circles in which he moved and endorsed by the Prince of Wales and others – that married men of his background were entitled to them. Thelma was distressed by them all, but particularly when her husband betrayed her throughout and after her first pregnancy. (Their son, a pilot in the RAF, was awarded a posthumous VC for his heroism in Libya during the Second World War.)

The twice-married Thelma, emotionally unsettled and drawn to men who either abused alcohol or abused her, was ready for a new relationship when, in early 1928, at the Furness's hunting-lodge at Burleigh Court near Melton Mowbray, Edward asked her to meet him in London. She left her husband and the other house guests to return to London specifically for the assignation. She had previously met the Prince of Wales in Scotland and later at a cattle market, the Leicester Livestock Fair. She did not need much persuading to become his mistress.

After rendezvousing with Thelma at York House, the Prince of Wales took her to dinner at the Hotel Splendide, where they dined and danced supposedly incognito. In the double autobiography she later wrote with her twin, Thelma described his 'shyness and charm' as contrasting overpower-ingly with the 'swaggering earthiness' of her husband. She had been waiting for a Prince Charming ever since she had discovered her husband's infi-delity, and was literally swept of her feet. She had never been able to trust any male. Her father was too distant a figure to have made any impression on her, and most men she had known had in one way or another let her down, either through alcoholism or philandering. She had fallen in love with Mar-maduke through mistaking his abusive aggression for strength, but now a real man – elegant, good-looking and one day to be the father of his people – had fallen in love with her. She could not have been happier. What she failed to recognize was that the charming and seductive Edward had acquired these characteristics as a child. Love had not been given him freely then, and as an adult he had to 'get round' women to obtain it.

The Furnesses had been planning a safari to Kenya, and it was fortuitous that it coincided with Edward's 1928 state visit. Edward and Thelma took full advantage of the relative privacy of the jungle to behave as if they were on their honeymoon. They made love under the stars, and Thelma described Kenya as their Garden of Eden. Their affair was almost discovered when, on the last day of the safari, the Prince collapsed with an attack of malaria while alone with her. He later recovered sufficiently to drive them to their destination before her husband returned.

Thelma became the official hostess at parties at Fort Belvedere, where she and Edward spent most weekends. While Edward's mother had taught him embroidery, Thelma now taught him *petit point*. It was home from home for the Prince, and he loved every minute of it. One weekend they were visited by Thelma's father, who read aloud while the two lovers sewed together.

Like most people whose parents had little time for them as children, the

Prince of Wales was obsessively punctual. He would be irritable and surly if he was kept waiting. On one occasion Thelma – always ready to indulge his foibles but knowing she was going to be late for their meeting – bought four tiny toy teddy bears, hoping to tease him out of his bad temper. The present was ideal. As a child Edward had loved his teddy, which he never let go of. On subsequent partings he and Thelma would exchange teddy bears as tokens of their affection.

Thelma had by now made up her mind to divorce Marmaduke, but she felt she had first to discuss her decision with her sister Gloria, who was in the United States. In January 1934 she put her lover in the care of her recently acquired good friend Wallis Simpson, who had courted her affection since they had been introduced to each other by Wallis's sister-in-law, Mrs Kerr-Smiley. Gloria approved of both the divorce and the Prince.

About two months later, on the voyage home, the excited almost thirty-year-old Thelma was surprised – and delighted – to find that the 23-year-old Aly Khan, one of the wealthiest men in the world, had also booked a passage on the *Bremen*. She found him exciting and attentive, and she certainly flirted with him, but whether she went to bed with him is not known – though, given the circumstances and her penchant for princes, it is more than likely that she did. The tall, dark and handsome Prince Aly Khan would certainly have been only too pleased to have usurped the short, fair and handsome Prince of Wales.

On returning to England and her lover, Thelma was surprised to see Wallis behaving familiarly with Edward at a party at Fort Belvedere. Though the Prince could be very friendly, he never permitted familiarity, and it soon became obvious that, in Thelma's absence, Wallis had taken her place. Confronted by Thelma later that evening, he denied any wrong-doing. But her beliefs were confirmed by his indifference to her distraught feelings, and she left the party, surrendering him to the so-called friend who, behind her back, had seduced him.

It was in Thelma's nature to expect rejection: it had been a familiar feature of her life. She was not surprised that the Prince had turned away from her. Indeed, she had in a sense set herself up for it, for she must have known that Edward would hear of her shipboard flirtation with Aly Khan. However, though she could hardly have known it, her fate was sealed less by this flirtation than by having left Edward in the care of Wallis Simpson. Wallis and Edward were already having a relationship before Thelma returned – and probably before she even set foot on the *Bremen*. Nevertheless, the American society hostess Elsa Maxwell was reflecting a popular view at the time when she wrote in 1937, as reported by Barbara Goldsmith in *Little Gloria . . . Happy at Last*, that 'Edward VIII might still be on the throne of England today, if not for Aly.'

Though by 1930 Frieda Dudley Ward had given way to Thelma Furness in Edward's affections, Frieda still exercised considerable influence over the Prince. 'I love and adore only you really, my darling,' he wrote to her in January 1932, and he still telephoned her nearly every day. (Such calls were known as 'the baker's calls' by Mrs Dudley Ward's domestic staff.) But her fall from grace was spectacular.

She had gradually disentangled herself from the Prince's most cloying attentions by claiming that the reputations of her children, of whom Edward was particularly fond, were at risk. During the autumn of 1934 she was preoccupied for some weeks with the health of her elder daughter, Penelope, who was seriously ill with appendicitis. On Penelope's recovery, Frieda telephoned York House only to be told by the embarrassed operator that there were now standing instructions that she was not to be put through. After sixteen years of an intimacy confirmed by his love-letters, Edward had ended the relationship in such a way that there could be no going back. It can only be assumed that Wallis Simpson had told him he must choose between Frieda and herself.

It was impossible for Frieda to stay in the relationship, and the Prince never saw her again. It was not in his nature to look back. All separations were painful for him, and he dealt with them by shutting his eyes. He could turn his back on his past as if it had never existed. He would in this way have 'forgotten' the many painful aspects of his childhood – his marginalization by his family; the loss of Mary Peters, the only woman who had adored him; the need to share Lala Bill with his younger brother; and, above all, his mother's cold indifference to his needs. He remembered them only by repeating them. There was occasional overlap between affairs, as if the previous mistress had to be kept on, like a spare wheel, to be used 'just in case'.

The Prince was unsure of himself and had never been able to cope emotionally with more than one woman at a time, though he was capable of ongoing flirtations with several. He was becoming depressed. He knew he had behaved badly towards Frieda Dudley Ward, but he felt he had had little choice. Encouraged by his friend Captain Edward 'Fruity' Metcalfe MC, he began misusing alcohol to cheer himself up.

Fruity was an Irish cavalry officer whom Edward had first met in about 1921. Born in Dublin of parents whose main interests were racing, he had entered Sandhurst in 1907 and left as a subaltern to join his regiment, the 3rd Skinner's Horse. He was serving in India when Edward, accompanied by Lord Louis Mountbatten and despondent at being separated from Frieda, arrived to carry out a tour. Fruity had initially been recruited to look after the polo ponies but was reassigned to become the Prince's aide-de-camp. The two soon became close friends. On their return to England his ADC introduced the Prince to the louche joys of Mayfair's nightlife. His Irish charm and engaging manner allowed him, without any objection from the Prince, to call Edward 'The Little Man' to his face. During the Prince's 1922 tour of the USA, Fruity caused a scandal when he left his wallet, containing several letters from the Prince, in the flat of a New York prostitute.

After the abdication Metcalfe, by then a major, was appointed as Edward's equerry. When the Second World War broke out, he and the Duke and Duchess of Windsor, as Wallis and Edward had become, were in France. Edward and Fruity had been the closest of friends for eighteen years, and hardly a day would pass when they were not together. Nevertheless, after cordial goodnights and assurances that they would see each other in the morning, suddenly, and without explanation, the Duke and Duchess departed for Biarritz, leaving Fruity to make his own way home. It was an abrupt and puzzling ending. First Frieda, then Thelma and then Fruity. Was Edward unable to cope with partings? In fact annihilating those on whom he was dependent, though violent, was utterly comprehensible given his upbringing.

Wallis Simpson, née Bessie Wallis Warfield, was born on 19 June 1896 at

Blue Ridge Summit, Monterey County, on the borders of Pennsylvania and Maryland. Her father, Teakle Wallis Warfield, born in 1870, was the son of a director of the Baltimore and Ohio Railroad and, like his father, a former state legislator. Wallis's mother, Alice Montague, born in 1871, was the daughter of an insurance salesman.

Wallis's parents' marriage was opposed by both families and was held quietly, with only the mandatory witnesses. The couple were married on 19 November 1895, and Wallis was born seven months later, though she always insisted that the wedding took place in June 1895 and that bureaucracy had slipped up by registering the marriage five months late. Wallis always resented the slurs cast on her legitimacy. (It is ironic that her greatest antagonist in the royal family was certainly the subject of such a bureaucratic lapse. The parents of Elizabeth Bowes-Lyon – the future wife of King George VI – neglected to register their daughter's birth within the proper time and had to pay a fine for their oversight.)

The absence of a properly validated birth certificate, and the confusion over the date of her parents' marriage, together with Wallis's occasional predilection for romanticizing the details of her life, later led to hostile speculation about her past, including rumours that she was conceived out of wedlock and, later, even that she was born male.

On 15 November 1896 Wallis's father died from tuberculosis, leaving her mother penniless. (Later in her childhood her mother would insist that, when she returned from school each day, Wallis must drink a tumbler of well-diluted blood squeezed from a steak, as a folk prophylaxis for tuberculosis.) Both her parents had claimed that they could trace their ancestry back to England. Her mother boasted that she was descended from the kings of the Isle of Man, the dukes of Manchester and the earls of Sandwich, and her father's ancestors were known to have held distinguished positions in the state government of Maryland before the American War of Independence. They told no one, however, that they had no money.

Her father's early death when she was only a few months old meant that Wallis never knew him, and the nature of his illness had prohibited any physical contact between them.

When her husband died, Wallis's mother.moved into her mother-in-law's house in Baltimore. This was also home to Teakle's brother, Solomon, who had never married but now fell in love with Alice, though his feelings were not reciprocated. Wallis was looked after by her mother with the help of an elderly Irish governess. Lacking the attentions of a father, she formed a strong attachment to Eddie, an elderly black servant and her Uncle Solomon's valet.

Wallis's early childhood was now strongly influenced both by the dominant personality of her grandmother and by the conflict between her grandmother and her mother. By the time she was five this conflict had become intolerable and, unable to stand the strain any longer, in 1902 Alice and her daughter moved out of the house, though Wallis would make return visits for dinner and at weekends.

Though Alice Warfield was supported financially by her brother-in-law, the monthly payments varied substantially in amount and she could never be sure of her financial position. She was forced to become a seamstress to make ends meet, until sometime in 1906 she was invited to live in Baltimore with her widowed sister, Bessie Merryman, the third female influence in Wallis's life.

Though Aunt Bessie later ran to fat, in her early middle age she was fashionable and elegant, with sufficient money to indulge her tastes. Unlike Wallis's mother she was also practical, with a strong trait of common sense which helped Alice to get her finances back on an even keel. When Alice finally achieved this she took a suite of rooms in an apartment block, where to supplement her income she began to cook for the other residents – until the cost of her extravagant menus outpaced the money she was paid. At this point Aunt Bessie stepped in again. Later accountss of this episode, such as that her mother ran a boarding-house, greatly angered Wallis.

Alice Warfield's fortunes gradually improved, and by the time her daughter began at Arundell Girls College in Baltimore in late 1906 she was able to move into a modest house in the town. Though it was Uncle Solomon who paid for Wallis's education at Arundell, her mother was disappointed rather than grateful for his help. She wanted her daughter to go to Bryn Mawr in Pennsylvania, an all-girls school with far greater snob appeal. She depended on the charity of her relatives, however, and had no say in the matter.

Wallis was an enthusiastic pupil, partly because of her intellectual curiosity but mainly because she wanted to impress her teachers and, above all, her uncle with her abilities. With no opposite-sex parent against whom to test her developing sexuality, she grew up with little sense of her own worth, but she knew from an early age that she wanted to be liked, and she did her best to be pleasing. Though she made some pretence at being interested in games, sports was not for her, and she would invent elaborate excuses to avoid strenuous physical activity, leading one teacher to recall years later, 'I have never known anyone who could so consistently for so many years so successfully evade the truth.' Wallis did not know what the truth was. She seemed to live in a fantasy world, peopled by men whom she could not identify but by whom she knew she wanted to be loved.

Soon after the move into a new house, Alice told her daughter that she intended to remarry. Her choice was John Rasin, a wealthy member of Baltimore's political élite. The news of the remarriage met with some hostility from Wallis, whose lack of experience of a father made her distrust men. On impulse, she destroyed the couple's wedding-cake while the civil ceremony was taking place. Having to share her only parent with a stranger was abhorrent to her, but, though she never called him by anything other than his surname, she eventually became quite fond of her stepfather.

The strong attachment to her uncle's valet, who had done his best to father her, was an aspect of her upbringing that cast its shadow over many of her later relationships with men. Women are known to be attracted to men who remind them of their fathers. In Wallis's case this would, in theory, mean that she would be attracted not to a reflection of the white father whom she had never known but to black men. Her relationships, however, tended to be with married men. Edward did not father a child and was only briefly father of his people. Had she turned him into a real father their sex life, contaminated by 'black' incestuous undertones, might well have ceased. As it was, her relationship with him was as intense on the day he died as it was when she first met him.

Alice's marriage to John Rasin ended with his death from Bright's disease in April 1913, when Wallis was almost seventeen. Her mother was unhinged by his death. Having lost her first husband to alcohol-related illness – largely self-inflicted – this new death was too great a blow and Alice too shocked to attend to the arrangements for the funeral and wake. Wallis had no problem in coping. But the trust-fund income which had supported Rasin during his lifetime had ceased with his death, and Wallis and her mother were once more impecunious.

Wallis had left Arundell in 1911 to board at Oldfields, a distinguished finishing-school in Maryland, leaving there just before her eighteenth birthday in the summer of 1914. For a few months, against the backdrop of distant war in Europe, Wallis attended the début parties of her friends. This was thanks to her Uncle Solomon, who by now was president of the Continental Trust Company, a merchant bank in Baltimore, and who provided the money for her ballgowns. Wallis's own début took place in December 1914.

By the time she was twenty Wallis knew that there had to be a man in her life. Shortly after the death of her beloved grandmother, Mrs Henry Warfield, her cousin Corinne Mustin introduced her to 26-year-old Win Spencer, whom she married almost at once. In 1916 Spencer was a lieutenant at the naval air station at Pensacola, Florida. Wallis's experience of waiting to hear the emergency gong that sounded at the base when an accident occurred, which was fairly often, led to a lifetime fear of flying. She had already lost two men in her life, her father and her stepfather, and she probably knew she would be unable to cope with the loss of another.

Win Spencer was an arrogant perfectionist – so obsessed with his work that he had little time for his wife. Like John Rasin, he was also a heavy drinker, and the depression later brought about by his younger brother's death in 1918, while flying over France, never left him. When drunk, Spencer would verbally, and sometimes physically, abuse Wallis.

She at first found it attractive that he commanded respect from the men, was authoritarian, and was six years older than she. But Wallis was not cut out for the life of a service wife, and her husband's psychological problems aggravated her distress. After his promotion to Assistant to Rear Admiral William Mofett in the US Department of the Navy in Washington, DC, their married life deteriorated dramatically and she resolved to leave him.

Her family, however, saw divorce as a social stigma and tried to dissuade her from going through with it. She was relieved when, early in 1922, Spencer was posted to China as commander of a gunboat. During his absence she became one of the leading lights of Washington society and fell deeply in love with Don Felipe Espil, an Argentinian diplomat. Felipe was everything her husband was not. He was educated and sophisticated, and during their two-year affair he instructed Wallis in the arts, food, literature and world politics. But she found herself becoming increasingly jealous, believing that his appearance at embassy functions exposed him to the charms of too many glamorous women, and when, finally, he had had enough of her possessive behaviour and gave her up she was heartbroken. Her reaction to this rejection shaped her attitude to all her later affairs. She persuaded her uncle to fund a trip to Europe in the summer of 1923 to cheer her up, and travelled with the recently widowed cousin who had introduced her to Win Spencer. After her cousin returned home Wallis stayed on in Paris, drinking too much, 'flirting' too much, and mourning the loss of the first real love of her life.

On her return to Washington, in June 1924, Wallis found that her 56-year-old mother had recently married for the third time. Her new husband, Charles Gordon Allen, was a legal executive in the Veterans' Administration. The news pleased Wallis. What did not please her was that Win wanted a reconciliation. With no money, no boyfriend and no reasonable alternative open to her, Wallis decided, despite her misgivings, to join him in Hong Kong. The long, slow journey via Hawaii, Guam and Manila gave her plenty of time to reflect on her marriage and whether there was any chance of salvaging it.

For a few days after her arrival all went well. Win told her that he had given up drinking, he looked well, and he behaved towards her with courtesy and love. But it did not last. He relapsed and began binge drinking again. Paranoid suspicions about her behaviour with other men further separated them. Wallis knew that she had to divorce him. She was told that she might obtain an easy divorce in the US Court for China in Shanghai, so she took a small steamer there from Hong Kong. On arrival she was advised by a local lawyer that divorce was costly and the process would be long, so she abandoned the purpose of her visit. While she was in Shanghai, however, she was introduced to Harold Robinson, a British diplomat, with whom she had a brief fling.

During her stay in the city, Wallis is said to have visited a harem in company with Marjorie, the mother of the Irish baronet Sir Jack Leslie. An article in the *Evening Standard* (10 June 2002) reported Jack's claim that Wallis learned the 'Shanghai grip', a sexual technique involving contraction of the muscles of the vagina and presumably used to control premature ejaculation. This would have endeared her to Edward who, it was claimed by Thelma Furness, suffered from this condition.

This trip to Shanghai gave rise to many rumours, all of which were later rehashed to present her in as bad a light as possible. There was later much talk about her sexual promiscuity on the steamer to Shanghai and about a mysterious 'China Dossier' supposedly compiled by MI5, which was said to have been circulated in British society, presumably to blacken her name at the time of the abdication. The dossier was also said to have mentioned sexual techniques she had supposedly learned while actually *working* in a Chinese brothel, involvement in drug running and espionage on behalf of the Soviet Union. The stories were crude in content and unlikely to have been accurate. Though the dossier almost certainly never existed, many thought that it did. There were, however, some elements of truth behind the rumours. After the initial period of reconciliation, Spencer had become increasingly volatile and had once beaten Wallis up so badly that she required medical treatment for damaged kidneys. When she asked him for a divorce, he is said to have dragged her off to a brothel and insisted that she watch him have sex with the prostitutes, threatening to kill her if she protested. This was the last straw, and Wallis packed her bags and took the train to Peking, where she thought that a friend at the US Legation would help her return to the USA without her having to ask for Win's help to do so. Another Navy wife who was to have accompanied her dropped out at the last minute, so Wallis travelled on her own, moving miraculously unscathed through a China in the grip of a bitter civil war, as General Sun Yat-sen attempted the overthrow of the government.

While in Peking she met an old friend, Katherine Bigelow, and fell in love with Katherine's new husband, Herman Rogers. Their affair is thought to have been platonic, but she remained in Peking with the couple for several months, becoming part of a presumably non-sexual but nevertheless bizarre *ménage à trois*. Herman remained one of her best friends even after her marriage to Edward, but years later he said that, though he admired her enormously, he had always thought of Wallis as utterly selfish. 'Even men she didn't want, she didn't want anyone else to have.' Wallis's insatiable need for the company of powerful males had probably begun with Win. She needed men who were not only potent but who also wielded power. Of the two, power seemed to have been the more important.

Wallis eventually travelled back to Shanghai, where she is rumoured to have had an affair with Count Galeazzo Ciano, the son-in-law of Benito Mussolini, by whom she is said to have become pregnant. The story runs that she had an abortion which was performed so badly that it left her with pelvic inflammatory disease and an inability to bear children.

That story is in contrast with another which could also explain her infertility. To coincide with the publication of *The Duchess of Windsor* in 1996, her biographer Michael Bloch wrote an article which alleged that there was some, albeit rather shaky, medical evidence that Wallis Simpson was in fact a man. Dr John Randall, a consultant psychiatrist at the Charing Cross Hospital and medical director of the Gender Reassignment Clinic, which assesses the suitability or otherwise of sex-change surgery for transsexuals, was said to have told Bloch that an unnamed colleague who had examined Mrs Simpson had given him this information. Dr Randall died in 1982, but some time later Bloch asked another psychiatrist at the hospital to explain what Randall could have meant. He was told that he must have been referring to a disorder called the androgen insensitivity syndrome. Men with this disorder look feminine – they have thick luxuriant hair, breasts and female external genitalia – but the vagina is abnormally short and the uterus and ovaries are absent. Penetrative sex would be almost impossible. Most patients with this disorder are brought up as females, and if Wallis Simpson suffered from this condition it might explain why she never had children.

However, in 1951 Wallis travelled to the United States for surgery. The press were told that she had 'cancer of the womb', and a hysterectomy was performed. Clearly if the hysterectomy story is correct then she could not have suffered from the androgen insensitivity syndrome, because there would have been no uterus to remove. Medical confidentiality would have prevented the surgeons discussing the case in public, but she either *did* have a uterus, in which case she was not a man, or the hysterectomy story was an invention to cover up a diagnosis such as pelvic inflammatory disease, which would have made coitus painful. The French doctor who attended the Duchess of Windsor throughout the final years of her life denied absolutely any suggestion that she was in any way *physically* sexually abnormal but understandably did not mention the strong possibility, given Wallis's many affairs, that she had suffered from a sexually transmitted disease.

In her youth realizing that she possessed only modest physical attributes – 'Nobody ever called me beautiful or even pretty,' she wrote in her memoirs – and partly because she could not afford the latest fashions, Wallis had taken to dressing in men's shirts and bow-ties in order to make an impact, and this later provided further fuel for speculation about her gender.

In 1926 in New York City, while waiting for her divorce from Spencer to be finalized, Wallis was introduced to the 29-year-old Ernest Aldrich Simpson, an Anglo-American former Guards officer and businessman. Simpson was good-looking, of military bearing, serious, intelligent, reserved, very knowledgeable in architecture and the arts and very witty. His marriage was already in trouble, and he and Wallis married in July 1928 after their respective divorces were settled. They lived initially in a furnished flat owned by Lady Chesham at 12 Upper Berkeley Street in London.

Simpson's sister was Maud Kerr-Smiley, who had introduced Edward to Frieda Dudley Ward. Though this gave Wallis an entrée into London society, she was ill at ease with English social customs and compensated by accentuating her American roots, making frequent references to her family's social standing in the Baltimore of her youth. The Simpsons moved to a new flat in Bryanston Court, where they began to entertain friends regularly and with such style that their invitations became much sought after. Among their guests were Benjamin Thaw, the first secretary at the American Embassy in London, and his wife, Consuelo, one of the Morgan family and sister of Thelma, Lady Furness, and Gloria Vanderbilt.

In January 1931 this relationship led to the Simpsons being invited to a

weekend hunting party organized by Thelma at her home in Melton Mowbray in Leicestershire, where the Prince of Wales would be present. Though
this first meeting was a difficult one for Wallis, who was still self-conscious
about her American mannerisms and unsure of how to behave in the presence of royalty, she rapidly cultivated her friendship with Thelma Furness,
though it is not clear if this was with the intention of ensnaring the Prince.
Wallis's cultivation of high-flyers suited her social ambitions, but they made
her very nervous. Nevertheless, her assiduity climaxed in her being presented to the King and Queen on 3 June 1931.

Simpson's business had been badly hit by the Depression that began in
1929, and it was some months after the first meeting before they met the
Prince again. During this time Wallis suffered from stomach ulcers and general poor health. (Wallis was never robust. In 1944, while she was in the
Unites States, she suffered an attack of severe abdominal pain that necessi-
tated the removal of her appendix. Following the operation, she was said to
have been that told she had stomach cancer – an unlikely diagnosis, since
she went on to live for another forty-two years. A more likely diagnosis is that
old adhesions from the inflammatory changes in her pelvis had caused
intestinal obstruction, presumably in the area of the appendix.)

The Prince's first invitation to the Simpsons to visit him at Fort
Belvedere occurred in January 1932. Thelma acted as hostess. Wallis was
very impressed if not with the Prince then at least with his home. She wrote:

> It was dark when we approached the Fort. Our headlights pick out a
> gravel driveway winding in graceful turns through a wood; suddenly
> there materialized a fascinating shadowy mass, irregular in outline
> and of different levels, the whole surmounted by a soaring tower
> bathed in soft light thrown up by concealed flood-lamps. Even before
> the car ground to a stop, the door opened and a servant appeared. An
> instant later the Prince himself was at the door to welcome his guests.

The invitations did not become regular until 1933, when she and Ernest
saw Edward on several occasions. Edward soon became a frequent visitor to
the Simpsons' flat, often staying talking with Wallis into the small hours

after Ernest had gone to bed. Then came the fateful day when Thelma Furness left her lover in Wallis's more than capable hands and the way became open for Wallis to supplant her friend in the Princes's affections.

Unlike with most of Edward's former mistresses, it had not been love at first sight. It is doubtful whether they even liked one another at first. Edward found himself only slowly falling in love with Wallis, but from 1934 he knew that he wanted to marry her. She soon rapidly rid his life of all previous involvements and showered him with attention, studying newspapers and the opinions of others so that she could speak knowledgeably about things that mattered to him. Even her defeated rival Thelma Furness thought there was something charismatic about her. Wallis herself could not accept that she was beautiful or even pretty – interestingly, given the doubts as to her sex in some quarters, she referred particularly to her male-like large hands, which she used awkwardly when she was making a point. At about the same time Sir Henry 'Chips' Channon, the American-born husband of Lady Honor Guinness and after 1935 a Member of Parliament, wrote in his diaries, 'she already has the air of a personage who walks into a room as though she expected to be curtsied to'.

Prince Edward's biographer Frances Donaldson reports that in 1936 Nancy Dugdale, whose husband was Stanley Baldwin's parliamentary private secretary, showed an example of Wallis's handwriting to a graphologist, Frau Gusti Oesterreicher. Frau Oesterreicher was unaware of the identity of the writer, but reported that she was

> A woman with a strong male inclination in the sense of activity, vitality and initiative, she must dominate, she must have authority, and without sufficient scope for her powers can become disagreeable . . . In the pursuit of her aim she can be most inconsiderate, and can hurt, but on the whole she is not without some instincts of nobility and generosity . . . She is ambitious and demands above all that her undertakings should be noticed and valued. In the physical sense of the word sadistic, cold, overbearing, vain.

Graphology is by no means an exact science, but Frau Oesterreicher seems to have arrived at conclusions with which many people would not argue. All his life the Prince of Wales had sought 'a woman with a strong male inclination'. He was made for domination, and Wallis was made to dominate.

By August 1934 the relationship had clearly crossed the boundary from flirtation to a full-blown love-affair when Edward invited Wallis to join him, without Ernest, on Lord Moyne's yacht *Rosaura* on a Mediterranean cruise. John Aird, the Prince's equerry, was certain that the *Rosaura* cruise was 'a turning point', and Wallis later stated in her autobiography that it was on this cruise that she and the Prince 'crossed the line that marks the indefinable boundary between friendship and love'. However, the Prince maintained that he and Wallis did not physically become lovers until after their marriage (he was probably referring to penetrative sex), and in 1937 he successfully sued the author Geoffrey Dennis for libel for insisting otherwise in *Coronation Commentary*.

At this time Ernest Simpson had no desire to leave his marriage and apparently balanced the perception of his being seen as a cuckold with the aura of importance that his wife's relationship brought. His views changed in 1935, when he refused to accompany Wallis and Edward on a skiing trip to Kitzbühel. Wallis insisted on going to Austria anyway and asked a friend of hers, Mary Kirk Raffray, to look after Ernest while he was in New York on business that autumn. This 'looking after' soon developed into an affair that marked the beginning of the end of the Simpsons' marriage.

It was during the winter of 1934, some months after Wallis had displaced Thelma, that Thelma Furness, Wallis Simpson and the Duchess of York (the former Elizabeth Bowes-Lyon) went skating together on the frozen pond of Windsor Great Park. Afterwards Wallis was scathing about the Duchess – calling her Cookie in private, because she was plump and ate too much, and ridiculing her to her face and behind her back. From then on the Duchess had no time for Mrs Simpson, and later she and her husband – by this time George VI – were implacable in their hostility towards her.

In January 1936, when 'the Empire's favourite son' was summoned by his mother to be at the Sandringham bedside of his dying father, relations between Wallis and the Prince of Wales came to a head. For a year the King had known of Edward's involvement with Mrs Simpson, and later it was said by Wallis's detractors that the news so distressed him that it hastened his death. The King seldom discussed emotions with his son or anyone else. He had asked Edward a few months earlier whether he was having a sexual relationship with Mrs Simpson, and Edward had vigorously denied it. (Was he, like President Clinton some sixty years later, speaking the truth, as he saw it, and assuming that only penetration counted as sex?)

King George V died peacefully at his home at Sandringham on 20 January 1936 at five minutes to midnight. Bulletins signed by his physicians, led by Lord Dawson of Penn, had been posted on the gates of Buckingham Palace from 18 January, so that anxious well-wishers could be kept informed of developments. The final bulletin was broadcast at midnight: 'Death came peacefully to the King at 11.55 p.m.' According to his critics, Lord Dawson had injected the already comatose King's jugular vein with cocaine and morphine so that the initial reports on his death would be provided by the morning newspapers rather than by the less prestigious evening ones.

The King had died with his family at his bedside. Queen Mary took her eldest son's hand and kissed it. She said, 'The King is dead; God save the King.' Edward wept. He had spent his life seeking the approval of his father, but had never achieved it – and now it was too late. His tears came from a mixture of sadness, panic at what lay ahead and perhaps relief. He had no longer to please his father. He was free. He could please himself.

Edward had spent the last few months contemplating marriage to Wallis. His intention was to take himself out of the line of succession and retire, possibly to his ranch in Canada. But indecision had caused him to drag his feet. He was now King Edward VIII and trapped by his constitutional duties. The British press was too deferential to report on Edward's affairs, and the general public – other than those few who read American newspapers – had no idea of the conflict that he now faced. He would have to choose between the throne and marriage to Wallis. His advisers had made it perfectly clear to him that he could not have both, though in his less sane moments he deluded himself that perhaps he could. His idea of a morganatic marriage – in which their progeny, if any (Wallis was now forty-one), would never inherit the throne after his death – was robustly turned down on the grounds that in English law there is no such thing as a morganatic marriage to a divorcee and that the lady whom he married would, by marrying the King, necessarily become Queen. On the morning after the death of his father, the new King was proclaimed by Garter King of Arms at St James's Palace.

It soon became clear that Edward's intention was to carry on as if nothing had changed, and he began to take a desultory interest in his constitutional duties, marking time while waiting for Wallis to divorce Ernest so that he could marry her. Everything had changed, however. Terrified of the step she was being asked to take and beginning to wonder whether she wouldn't be happier if she stayed with Ernest, Wallis decided at the end of February 1936 to spend a few days in Paris on her own.

While she was away, the King and Ernest met to discuss the situation. Ernest's view was that Wallis would have to choose between them. But Edward's response – 'Do you think I would be crowned without Wallis by my side?' – seemed to settle the matter, and when Wallis returned to London she was furious to find that two men had, behind her back, decided her future for her. Wallis's idea was that she stay with Ernest and at the same time remain the King's mistress.

Edward had insisted that Ernest should shoulder the burden of responsibility then required under English divorce law. So Ernest obligingly spent a night – or at least shared breakfast in bed on 21 July 1936 – with a lady by the name of 'Buttercup' Kennedy at the Hôtel de Paris in Bray, thereby providing the necessary evidence of adultery for the detectives whom Wallis had engaged to follow him.

Beginning to tire of his unaccustomed constitutional duties, Edward decided it was time for a holiday, and in the summer of 1936 he paid what today would be more than £250,000 to charter the spectacular 250-foot, 1,391-ton yacht *Nahlin* from Lady Yule, having turned down the loan of the Duke of Westminster's yacht on the grounds that it was not smart enough. He and Wallis, together with many of their friends, cruised along the Dalmatian coast via Greece to Turkey.

It was clear to all those who welcomed them in their many ports of call that Wallis and the King were in love and that neither of them cared who knew it. Rumour had it that they had consummated their relationship on the cruise. However, a sour note was sounded by Lady Diana Cooper, wife of Duff Cooper, later the 1st Viscount Norwich. Philip Ziegler quotes her as saying, 'The truth is she's bored stiff with him, and her picking on him, and her coldness towards him, far from policy, are irritation and boredom.'

After the cruise ended in early September, Edward returned by air to London and Wallis went to Paris for a few days. Suffering from a fever, she lay in bed in the Hôtel Meurice reading the American papers. She was horrified by the amount of press coverage her relationship with the King was attracting and, terrified that she would be unable to cope with the fallout from it, she panicked and 'decided' she did not want to marry him after all. She wrote what was intended to be a farewell letter to Edward: 'I really must return to Ernest – we are so awfully congenial and understand getting on together very well – I know Ernest and have the deepest affection and respect for him. I feel I am better with him than with you. I want you to be happy. I feel sure I can't make you so and I honestly don't think you can me.'

But her last-minute attempt to change her destiny was doomed to failure. By July 1936 Ernest had already moved out of the marital home and was living with Mary Kirk Raffray. He was no longer prepared to put up with increasingly outspoken public ridicule in mainly American newspapers over his wife's behaviour. (In November 1936 *Time* magazine reported that he was to be asked to perform in a play called *The Unimportance of Being Ernest*, in which he would supposedly recite the line 'My only regret is that I have but one wife to lay down for my King.') He had made his decision. The option of returning to him was no longer open.

When Edward received Wallis's letter he telephoned her threatening to cut his throat if she did not return to him at once. She felt she had no option and, accompanied by Herman and Katherine Rogers, she returned to England. Edward, who was at Balmoral, drove himself to Aberdeen to meet her off the train from London on 23 September. He had been expected to open a new hospital in the city on the same day, and he provoked a minor political row, though a major one in Aberdeen, by asking the Duke of York to stand in for him.

The divorce petition was due to be heard on 27 October, and Wallis was finding change too frightening. She clung to the delusion that she could remain the King's mistress until a more acceptable candidate for the post of Queen came along. A letter she wrote to the new King just before the court hearing, though sugary in its content, neatly put the responsibility for what was quickly becoming a fiasco on to her lover's shoulders. She told Edward that they had stirred up a hornet's nest and that she was worried about coping with the huge upheaval that was likely to occur in her life. (She may well have been right to doubt that Edward would be able to fulfil her emotional needs. Within a few years of their eventual marriage, Wallis's name became linked with that of the bisexual playboy Patrick Donahue, known to his friends as 'Jimmy', an heir to the Woolworth fortune.)

A few weeks later, her doubts, if indeed doubts there were, had evaporated. In another slightly panicky letter written by her to the King after a night of deep discussion with her friends George and Kitty Hunter and just before the court hearing, Wallis applied pressure through false insistence that Edward should do what was best. None the less there was an anxious sting in its tail: 'Do please say what you think is best for all concerned when you call me after reading this. Hold me tight, please David.' (Edward was known as David by his intimates and his family.)

She also telephoned the King from Normandy, where she had been sent to cool the situation. Diana Vreeland reports an account by one of Edward's attendants of a further exchange at odds with reality in which Wallis insisted, 'You will never ever see me again. I will be lost in South America. *Never* leave your country. You *cannot* give in! You can *not*! You were *born* to this – it is your heritage, it is *demanded* of you by your country by the traditions of nine hundred years.'

Throughout her life Wallis had always taken the dominant role in her relationships. The little-girl role did not suit her. Her father's early death was indelibly stamped on her psyche, and her experience as a small child provided her with few if any expectations that men would stay with her. When men promised to honour, love and comfort women, she did not believe them. If, as now, they did not abandon her she tried to set up situations in which it became impossible for them to stay with her. Wallis's underlying anxiety had always demanded that she be in control of events and therefore of herself. When she was controlled by events she panicked. Morbid fears of loss persisted throughout her life. Her mind was in conflict. She needed Edward and she depended on him, but she could not tolerate being controlled by him. She tried to explain to Edward on the telephone why she wanted to protect him. When she told him that she did not want him to renounce his throne, his reply shocked her. He told her that 'the only conditions on which I can stay here are if I renounce you for all time, and this of course I will not do'.

It was obviously essential that Wallis's divorce should become absolute before the King abdicated his throne. If her divorce petition failed (it was just possible that it might be claimed that she and Ernest had – illegally – colluded in citing adultery with 'Buttercup' Kennedy), then the King would not have to abdicate. Much to the disappointment of the authorities, however, collusion could not be proved. Instead, the day after the divorce hearing there was some last-minute discussion between senior members of the Cabinet and Wallis's solicitor as to how much 'she would take to clear out'. Neville Chamberlain, the Chancellor of the Exchequer, wrote in his diary that Wallis was an unscrupulous woman who did not love the King but was merely after his money. Wallis's solicitor, Theodore Goddard, on whose acumen she had come to depend, discussed with her the wisdom of marrying the King. Wallis was now so anxious that it would have been a great relief to her if the situation could revert to the status quo ante. She agreed to withdraw the divorce petition, but it is not clear whether she was telling the truth or was in such a panic that she would have agreed to anything. She was so distraught at the crisis she had brought about that she said she would be willing to leave Edward but also stated that, no matter where she went, the King would follow her.

She permitted Goddard to draw up a press statement to the effect that during the past few weeks 'Mrs Simpson has invariably wished to avoid any action or proposal which would hurt or damage His Majesty or the throne.' Her solicitor also announced that he had discussed withdrawal of the divorce petition with his client, who had expressed her willingness to do so. He confirmed that such a course was Mrs Simpson's genuine and honest desire and that she would do anything to prevent the King from abdicating.

The note was signed by Goddard and countersigned by Lord Brownlow, an old friend of Edward's.

The country, at last aware of the situation, was becoming increasingly hostile to the King's decision to abdicate if the Church forbade a marriage between a sovereign and a divorced woman with whom everyone believed he had committed adultery. Leo Amery MP convinced himself that he spoke for the vast majority of the House of Commons as well as the country when he said that the nation was 'shocked that the King could hesitate between his duty to the throne and his affection for a second-rate woman'. As a friend recalled to Wallis's biographer Greg King, 'I think that ultimately she felt very, very betrayed by the abdication. She rarely spoke about that period of her life but once she did admit that the Duke's abdication had hurt her terribly.' She seemed to be saying that had she been more fully informed of the constitutional, moral, religious and political events that had determined Edward's decision she would have better known what to do. According to Greg King in *The Duchess of Windsor*, 'She was more than a little put out at having her future essentially determined for her', though she genuinely felt guilty about causing a crisis that threatened the stability of the monarchy.

Only two major public figures, Winston Churchill in Parliament and Lord Beaverbrook in the press, had spoken up for Edward. Beaverbrook wanted to see Edward on the throne and his marriage postponed to a time when the public had got used to the idea. Churchill said that if the King pushed for a morganatic marriage, despite constitutional law, he would support him, but the Prime Minister, Stanley Baldwin, said if the King did follow such a course the government would resign. To heighten the tension still further, Wallis again developed cold feet about marrying and received assassination threats.

It was Geoffrey Dawson, the editor of *The Times*, who finally brought the crisis to a head by suggesting on 8 December that Edward's actions were doing untold damage to the British throne. On 10 December 1936, 326 days after he had been proclaimed King, Edward was left with no alternative but to sign the Instrument of Abdication, placing his throne in the uncertain hands of his unprepared and socially anxious brother Bertie. Leaving his country in the aptly named HMS *Fury*, Edward travelled from France to

Vienna to stay in a country house lent to him by Baron Eugene de Roths-
child and his wife Kitty – prompting anti-Semitic comments from some
sections of the Austrian aristocracy.

It was not until 3 May 1937 that Wallis obtained the decree absolute.
Edward had been without her for the loneliest five months of his life. Roths-
child was also pleased when the decree absolute came through, because,
according to Wallis, Edward passed the time by having a brief affair with
Kitty.

Wallis could hardly have been more traumatized by the events leading
up to the abdication, her vilification in the British press, Edward's break
with almost every member of his family, and the anxious wait for the divorce
proceedings to be finalized. Before Ernest had finally left her for Mary Kirk
Raffray, for over five months she had hovered between the proverbial two
stools. Would Edward change his mind, and if so would it be too late to dissuade Ernest from divorcing her? She was now trapped in another five
months' time warp and there could be no going back. She panicked. Her
ability to control events had ceased to exist, and paranoid thoughts surfaced.
She felt that the world had turned against her, and in her more depressed
moments she may have thought that even Edward had done so too. No one
loved her. No amount of reassurance by Edward – her lifeline to sanity –
could help. She suspected everyone. Her anxiety diminished only when her
solicitor telephoned her with the news for which she had been waiting, and
it did not disappear entirely until she and the Duke of Windsor – as Edward
was now to be titled – were together at last and planning the wedding. A
week later Edward left the Austrian castle for a French one. He and Wallis
were now the guests of Charles Bedaux at the Château de Candé at Tour-
raine.

Throughout their separation Edward's anxiety was also at a high level.
He had come to hate every member of his family. His mother had said that
he would be permitted to return to England only for her funeral, and of his
three brothers only the Duke of Kent did not turn against him. The Archbishop of Canterbury, the reactionary Cosmo Lang, speaking on the radio,
declared that 'the promise of his service as Prince of Wales [had been] ruined
by his disastrous liking for vulgar society, and by his infatuation for this Mrs

Simpson'. Edward was even more affronted by a letter from his brother Bertie, who informed him that it would not be possible for any of the family to attend the wedding and went on to state his belief that 'the vast majority of people are as strongly as ever opposed to a marriage which caused a King of England to renounce the throne'. With only a few friends present, the Duke married Wallis on 3 June 1937 at the Château de Candé, with Fruity Metcalfe as his best man and with the service conducted, despite the objections of the Archbishop of Canterbury, by the Reverend Robert Anderson Jardine, vicar of a church in County Durham.

The lawyer Walter Monckton, one of Edward's few remaining supporters, took the Duchess of Windsor aside after the wedding and told her that she was disliked in England for taking the people's King away from them, but if in the end she made him happy all that hostility would evaporate. If she made him unhappy, however, nothing would be too bad for her. The Duchess promised that she would do her best, and until she met Jimmy Donahue she undoubtedly did.

The Duke never gave up hope that at some point he and Wallis would be invited to return to England. Not only did the invitation never come, however, but Edward had to put up with ongoing hostility expressed by his mother, by his brother King George VI and his sister-in-law Queen Elizabeth. After the Second World War the one-time Prince of Wales and enthroned – though uncrowned – King Edward VIII of England lived out his life as an exile in France. But, though the Duke's family may have elected to deny his existence, his former subjects did not. When their 'little boy lost' and former King returned to his homeland in a coffin, thirty-six years after he had left it, 60,000 men and women came to pay their respects and to have a last glimpse of their immensely popular and charismatic former monarch as he lay in state at Windsor.

Wallis Simpson's addictive need for men to admire her had manifested itself in multiple sexual liaisons before she met Edward, and it may have surfaced again in Palm Beach, Florida, in the late 1940s, when she and Edward became involved with the playboy Jimmy Donahue.

Jimmy had been born in Palm Beach in 1915 and was immensely wealthy, being an heir to the Woolworth fortune through his mother, Jessie, and to a fat-rendering business through his father, James Patrick Donahue. His father was a bisexual philanderer, addicted to gambling, drugs and drink, and he squandered much of his wife's fortune on all three. (On the day of their wedding, Jessie's father, F.W. Woolworth, had wept in his office for most of the morning.) He committed suicide by swallowing poison in front of two of his sons when losing at a poker game. At the time, Jessie was in a private clinic suffering from a 'nervous breakdown'.

Jimmy was never fully educated, since his doting mother would keep him at home with her whenever she felt she needed his company. She preferred Jimmy to her older son, and because she had wanted a girl she not only brought him up as a girl but also often dressed him as one.

Donahue grew up bright, witty and superficially sociable. As soon as he managed to escape from his oppressive home life he became notorious for the number of affairs he had with both men and women in his family's social circle. His partners ranged from the much respected Francis Spellman, Cardinal of New York, to Lupe Velez, known as the Mexican Spitfire, an outrageous actress of squalid habits who caused Gary Cooper (one of her boyfriends) to have a mental breakdown when she left him to marry the first screen Tarzan, Johnny Weissmuller. Donahue also had an affair with Libby Holman, a nightclub torch singer who was suspected of killing her husband, Zachary Smith Reynolds, heir to the R.J. Reynolds tobacco fortune, but who was said to have escaped prosecution because the Reynolds family preferred not to have the events surrounding the case aired in public. The well-known actress Martha Raye and *Call Me Madam* star Ethel Merman were also on his hit list. Philip Ziegler described him as an 'epicene gigolo'.

Jimmy had a strange relationship with his cousin Barbara Hutton, the heiress granddaughter of F.W. Woolworth, who in 1933, when she was twenty-one, inherited her mother's $50 million estate. She underwrote Jimmy's living expenses, and he accompanied her and the first two of her seven husbands on their respective honeymoons. Through Barbara's wealth and his own social connections, Jimmy entered a level of society that might otherwise have been barred to him. In 1931 Barbara had been introduced to the Prince of Wales, who invited her to spend some time with his party at Biarritz. Famous because of the family into which he had been born, Jimmy Donahue later harboured fantasies about becoming the best friend of the Duke of Windsor.

During most of the Second World War the Duke was governor-general and commander-in-chief in the Bahamas, and towards the end of the war Wallis became friendly with Jessie Woolworth Donahue, Jimmy's mother. The Duke liked Jimmy's older brother, Woolworth, but when he first met Jimmy, at Palm Beach during the same period, he did not take to him. However, having been brought up by his 'chaffing' father to appreciate humour which discomfited others, he was amused by Jimmy's practical jokes, which were often reported in the press. Donahue once wrote a long lyrical letter to Mrs Harry Hays Morgan, the mother of Lady Thelma Furness, to the effect that Palm Beach, where he spent much of his time partying, missed her presence. The final page had 'SO GET YOR FAT OLD WRINKLED ASS DOWN HERE' scrawled in large capital letters. On one of Barbara Hutton's honeymoons he urinated on a crowd of Fascists from the balcony of her hotel in Rome while shouting 'Viva Haile Selassie! Long Live Ethiopia!', then hid under his cousin's bed. When the police failed to find him, because Barbara had said that she had not seen him, he called out 'She's not telling the truth' and was arrested and expelled from the country. Later he performed a similar stunt in Berlin, calling out 'Down with Hitler!' and was chased through his hotel's revolving doors several times before being caught.

The affair – if indeed it existed – between Donahue and Wallis would probably have started during a voyage of the *Queen Mary* to Cherbourg from New York which the Windsors and Donahue began in May 1950, when Jimmy was thirty-four and Wallis twenty years his senior. The three of them spent the remainder of the summer in Paris, mostly in each other's company. It was assumed that Jimmy and Wallis were lovers because Donahue – usually when under the influence of chemicals – claimed they were, though for obvious reasons the minutiae of their love life which he detailed could be neither confirmed nor denied.

In the light of other evidence concerning the Duchess of Windsor's expression of obvious affection for Donahue, an affair would seem unlikely, for Jessie Donahue was largely bankrolling the Windsors, and his mother threatened to cut Jimmy off without a penny if he brought about a divorce from the Duke. The Windsors' own constant money worries would also have discouraged a split between Jimmy and his sources of income, since a Donahue–Wallis liaison would have been penniless from the start.

The end came in 1954, during a visit by the Windsors to Germany. At a private dinner, Wallis complained that Donahue's breath stank of garlic. In a fit of rage fuelled by the Windsors' greed over the money that his family supplied, by his contempt for the Duke and by the hatred he was beginning to feel for Wallis – he later claimed that he had to put a bandage over his eyes when he made love to her – he kicked her shin so hard under the dinner table that he drew blood. Enraged, the Duke attended to his wife's injury then turned to Donahue and, according to the Windsors' biographers J. Bryan III and Charles Murphy, said, 'We've had enough of you, Jimmy. Get out!'

Twelve years later, in September 1966, alone in a Fifth Avenue hotel room in New York, Jimmy Donahue died choking on his own vomit after an overdose of Seconal, a barbiturate sleeping-pill. At this stage publicist Guido Orlando, whose job it had been to protect the Windsor's reputations in the Bahamas during the war, confided to Charles Higham, the Duchess of Windsor's biographer, that the Duke and Jimmy Donahue had concocted an elaborate smokescreen to hide their own love-affair.

Allegations of the Duke's homosexuality were also made by Norman Lockridge in *Lese Majesty: The Private Lives of the Duke and Duchess of Windsor,* but there was no confirmation of this by other contemporary biographers or in the diaries of his friends or attendants. The author Michael Thornton, however, reports Noël Coward as having said to Truman Capote that 'He pretends not to hate me but he does, and its because I'm queer and he's queer but unlike him I don't pretend not to be.'

In *Abdication* Christopher Warwick also maintains that the Duke was a repressed homosexual. Stories have also circulated that he was impotent and in addition suffered from premature ejaculation – a possibility given his impulsiveness and his excessive preoccupation with time. In her autobiography, *The Honeycomb*, Adela Rogers St John claimed that Wallis had told her that Edward had an inordinately small penis, and one of Edward's friends is said to have stated that 'all of the sons of George V have small penis complexes'. This is 'corroborated' in Ralph G. Martin's *The Woman He Loved,* where an unnamed 'friend' of the Duke is quoted as saying:

> To put it bluntly he had the smallest pecker I have ever seen. Can you
> imagine what that did to him? Here are all these beautiful woman all
> over the world, all ready and willing to go to bed with the Prince
> Charming of the world, all of them expecting the most eventful
> romantic night of their lives. And the ones who made it with him, can
> you imagine their disappointment? And can you imagine how he felt?

One can speculate that Edward was a masochist who enjoyed being
beaten as a result of an upbringing with a harsh father and with a surrogate
mother, the sadistic Mary Peters, who hurt him and then consoled him. As
an adult he may well have re-enacted with other women the pain of suffering and the joy of comforting attention that followed on from it. The Duke
may have found in the dominant Wallis Simpson an acceptable substitute
for a male lover. A child who has been brought up by a harsh father may, as
an adult, seek male love as compensation. Despite his numerous heterosexual affairs, Edward did seem to have had an underlying hostility to
women. Only Wallis Simpson stood the course. Every other woman in his
life was used and then abandoned.

Other stories of bizarre or unusual sexual tastes – including infantilism,
dominance and foot fetishism – have also been circulated. In his biography
of the Duchess, Greg King reports that, in interviews he conducted, it was
even alleged that Wallis had to resort to a strap-on dildo to provide the Duke
with sexual satisfaction. One story in particular appears to have gained
popular currency: Wallis was said to exercise on the Duke some obscure
Chinese sexual techniques. In *Edward VIII* Frances Donaldson has the last
word on all this. She remarks on the irony that 'It might be true to say that
during the whole of his youth the Prince was criticized for over-indulgence
in the sexual act while ever since he was believed incapable of it until he met
his wife.'

When the turmoil surrounding Edward's abdication and his sexual philandering had faded, and the Second World War had come to an end, the
more thoughtful of his subjects were relieved that his younger brother – the

straightforward, unreservedly patriotic King George VI, a happily married husband and loving father to his children – had, with not a hint of scandal attached to his name, seen the country through one of the most painful and difficult times in its history, and in so doing had helped restore his people's faith in the monarchy.

Edward had grown up believing in discipline, mistaking his father's weakness in this respect as strength. As a young man he, like many others, had been of the opinion that Adolf Hitler was a great leader, and he may have felt that Hitler's emphasis on blond hair and blue eyes qualified him to be a better father than his own, who had never commented on his son's Nordic good looks. Later, Edward was also said to have been impressed by Hitler's promise to restore him to the throne after eliminating the hostile elements in England who opposed him. Many who knew Edward well were certain that, had Hitler been able to meet him in the early stages of the war, he would have agreed *not* to have been restored to the throne but to become the leader of a republic favourable to German interests.

Had the Prince of Wales not met Wallis Simpson, would his Nazi sympathies have allowed him to ally himself with the Munich appeasers when he became King? Had Hitler defeated a largely unprepared Britain, would he have rewarded his protégé by appointing him governor of a newly created republic? Perhaps we owe Wallis Simpson more than we realize.

Charles, Prince of Wales

'When You Are King, Dilly Dilly . . . '

Like all other members of the royal family, Prince Charles, the Prince of Wales, is required to conform to the provisions of the 1772 Royal Marriages Act. This act, introduced by King George III, was aimed at protecting the royal bloodlines of the House of Hanover. Its essential provision was – and still is – to prevent any member of the royal family under the age of twenty-five from marrying without the permission of the sovereign. If a member over the age of twenty-five wished to marry a Catholic, he or she has to give notice to the Privy Council and would lose their right of succession and also their other royal privileges. They would then be free to marry if both Houses of Parliament gave their consent. (George III, while disapproving of the sexual behaviour of his sons, unwittingly gave them the green light to behave as badly as they wished with their *mistresses*, because he knew that any promises of marriage made by his sons would be declared null and void under the terms of the act.) The act had been preceded in 1701 by the Act of Settlement, which did not forbid a member of the royal family from marrying a Catholic but prevented anyone who did so from acceding to the throne.

On 4 November 1952, nine months after the death of her father, Queen Elizabeth II declared under oath that she was a faithful Protestant, and at her coronation on 2 June 1953 she promised that she would 'maintain the Protestant reformed religion in the United Kingdom'. In 1985, because of this oath, she forbade the Prince and Princess of Wales from attending a Papal Mass at the Vatican.

Not only may Catholics – and divorced women – not become the sovereign's consort, a princess of royal blood is the preferred option for the marriage of a male heir. In the absence of a suitable princess, well-born commoners of impeccable character may be considered. The House of Windsor's longest-standing commoner, Queen Elizabeth the Queen Mother, who came into the family with the best of credentials and married the future King George VI, remains the yardstick against which all recent potential spouses have been measured. The Queen Mother, who died in 2002 at the age of 101, and her late husband were royals about whom there was never a breath of sexual scandal.

Recent royal marriages, such as those of Princess Margaret and Lord Snowdon, Prince Andrew and Sarah Ferguson, the Princess Royal and Captain Mark Phillips, which began as love-matches, have none the less failed. Is there a possibility that marriages arranged for dynastic reasons are more stable than those based either on love or on the need to re-enact a failed relationship with a parent in the hope of righting ancient wrongs? Would Prince Charles have been happier had he married a suitable princess, such as Marie-Astrid of Luxembourg with whom his name was linked but with whom he was not in love, rather than Lady Diana Spencer?

The answer is probably yes. Sovereigns who have believed that they have found a 'mother' in a woman who loved them have been destined to perpetuate rather than resolve their childhood problems. Disappointment has followed disappointment. So desperate was Henry VIII to rid himself of Catherine of Aragon, with whom he had fallen in love at their first meeting, that he divorced his country from the Church of Rome, having been refused permission by the Pope to divorce his wife so that he could marry his mistress, the presumably more fertile Anne Boleyn. King Edward VII fell in love at first sight with Princess Alexandra, but three children later their love-affair was over. George V, however, whose marriage could not have been more arranged, since he took on the responsibility of marrying his dead brother's fiancée, grew fond of his wife and remained by her side until they were separated by his death. Was this because he was so much in love with his mother that a limited and mainly procreational relationship with another woman was his only option?

Permission for the sovereign to marry cannot be taken for granted. King Edward VIII discovered this to his cost when the Archbishop of Canterbury and Queen Mary, backed up by his brother George, who was later to inherit his throne, denied him his wish to marry the twice divorced Wallis Simpson if he wanted to remain on the throne.

While candidates for a male royal hand must not have 'a past', candidates for the hand of a female royal are not bound by this restriction. When Princess Elizabeth married Prince Philip and Lady Diana Spencer married Prince Charles, the husbands were not asked whether or not they had been involved in premarital sex. The author Christopher Wilson mentions a story (to which he ascribes no sources) that Prince Philip had in fact been invited by the writer Daphne du Maurier to spend the weekend at her home in Cornwall just before his wedding to Princess Elizabeth in 1947. According to Wilson's account, the weekend culminated in Philip saying that he did not want to leave du Maurier. Daphne du Maurier was married to General 'Boy' Browning, who was one of the architects of the September 1944 Arnhem drop aimed at establishing a bridgehead over the Rhine before the Allied invasion of Europe. Browning was an equerry to Princess Elizabeth's father, King George VI, and thought it his duty to point out to Prince Philip that Daphne was fourteen years his senior and that there would be an almighty scandal if he did not do his duty to the country. The interlude seems to have been grist to du Maurier's literary mill, because the name of the hero/narrator of her next novel, *My Cousin Rachel*, published in 1951, was Philip.

Prince Philip's Uncle George, the second Marquess of Milford Haven and brother of Lord Louis Mountbatten, owned one of the country's largest collections of pornography, which he kept at his home at Lynden House, near Maidenhead. The adolescent Philip was a frequent visitor to the house, since his Uncle George and Aunt Nadejda (Countess Torby) had effectively served as father and mother figures to him when his own father, the playboy Prince Andrew of Greece, proved ineffectual. (Prince Andrew had been imprisoned and then exiled when his brother, the King, was deposed in 1922. His cousin King George V intervened with the Greek military dictator General Pangalos, and the naval cruiser HMS *Calypso* was sent to rescue the family. Prince Andrew abandoned his family soon after, and the year-old Philip and his four older sisters were left to bring themselves up while their father enjoyed the distractions of life on the French Riviera.) It is highly likely that Philip, like any other boy of his age, would have spent some time in his uncle's library satisfying his sexual curiosity. Throughout his marriage, however, Prince Philip, possibly having successfully satisfied this – has been the self-appointed guardian of what he has seen as the rectitude of royal life and the royal family's most resolute defender.

When, in 1953, the 22-year-old Princess Margaret fell in love with the divorced royal equerry Group Captain Peter Townsend, the royal family closed ranks. The Princess was told that if she waited until she was twenty-five and then still wished to marry she would be permitted to do so on condition that she renounce her right of succession and forfeit all her other royal privileges. These sanctions, coupled with pressure from the Church, led her to make a poignant statement that she would give up Townsend. In the vanguard of those who pressed hardest for her rejection of the equerry was her holier-than-thou brother-in-law, Prince Philip.

Paradoxically, Philip himself mixed with many of the sexiest photographic 'models' of the 1940s and 1950s through his regular visits to his friend Baron, the court photographer responsible for the royal wedding pictures in 1952, whose studio was purported to have been the venue for numerous illicit assignations. Philip was also a member of the Thursday Club (later renamed the Monday Club), whose lunches at Wheeler's Restaurant in Old Compton Street he regularly attended. The club achieved notoriety for the drunken rowdiness of its members, one of whom, Dr Stephen Ward, introduced call-girl Christine Keeler to, among others, the Secretary of State for War, John Profumo. At the same time as her affair with Profumo, Christine Keeler was sexually involved with a Soviet KGB agent who, during 'pillow talk', was inadvertently fed sensitive sexual material relating to the British royals. The sorry situation ended with the fall of the Macmillan government in 1963 and the suicide of Stephen Ward.

There have been rumours of a romantic friendship between Philip and Merle Oberon. According to Charles Higham's biography of the actress, in 1953 Philip insisted that the royal yacht *Britannia* sail past her Acapulco cliff-top house with the Royal Marines band playing some of her favourite tunes on deck. Gossip has also linked his name with the actress Pat Kirkwood – 'Britain's answer to Betty Grable' – to whom he was introduced by

Baron, with whom she had been romantically involved. After a late-night party with Kirkwood following a show at the London Hippodrome during his wife's first pregnancy, Prince Philip was said to have been formally rebuked by King George VI. According to so-called royal watchers, Philip is also thought to have had a child by the actress Hélène Cordet, whom he had known since boyhood.

But when Philip first met Elizabeth he had undoubtedly fallen in love with her. His background demanded it. After his father had defected to the pleasures of Monte Carlo's nightlife, Philip had been largely brought up by his four much older sisters, the youngest seven years older than he, with his mother, Princess Alice of Battenberg, hardly featuring in this. Princess Alice was profoundly deaf, and Philip's later relationships with women, both before and after he met Princess Elizabeth, echoed what he must have believed as a child: that his mother never listened to him. But he did not have to shout when he met Princess Elizabeth. She listened, and he fell in love with her. Since then Philip has learned to deal with his fear of being ignored by being provocative, and his so-called gaffes are widely reported.

Why is it that women with a past are disqualified from marrying into the royal family, but men with a past are not? Why are men who have affairs designated as 'lovers', while women are demeaned as 'mistresses'? Could her past be the reason why Camilla Parker Bowles has been ostracized by the Queen, who has visited her eldest son's home only twice in fourteen years? If keeping a mistress had stood in the way of a sovereign making a suitable marriage, the monarchy would have come to an end long ago. The Royal Marriages Act as it stands discriminates against women. The only possible argument for the double standards of this discrimination is that a royal bride could arguably already be pregnant by another man and subsequently give birth to an heir who is not of royal blood. When Prince Charles met Lady Diana Spencer it was well understood that there was no risk of any contravention of the Royal Marriages Act. Diana had never been married, she was not a Catholic, and her ancestry and good character made her in every respect a suitable candidate for the role of the Princess of Wales. So the Queen gave her son permission to marry her.

Diana's early life had been spent trying to come to terms first with the breakdown of her parents' marriage, then with her anorexia and bulimia, and above all with her low self-esteem, contributed to by having been abandoned as a six-year-old when her parents divorced. When Prince Charles proposed marriage, she must have felt that her emotional needs would now stand a chance of being fulfilled. She had not taken into account – and how could she? – that Charles was every bit as needy as she was. Like her, he had to all intents and purposes come from what was a broken home. As a child he would have seen his parents as happily married, with time for one another and time for their royal duties. It would not be until much later that he would recognize that their responsibilities left little time either for him or for his siblings.

Prince Charles was born on 14 November 1948. His relationship with his parents ran into trouble almost immediately after the premature death of his 57-year-old grandfather King George VI. The close family unit then began to crumble as Charles's parents were often absent while fulfilling their constitutional duties. Charles and his younger sister, Princess Anne, had previously been separated from their parents from time to time when such duties took Elizabeth and Philip away from home, but their upbringing at Clarence House and Windsor Castle had been relatively normal. Though they both had nannies, their parents were only too happy to play with them and attend personally to their needs, unlike their emotionally remote great-grandparents, King George V and Queen Mary, who had been content to leave their children almost entirely in the care of servants.

In late 1951 a major separation took place. Princess Elizabeth and Prince Philip left England for a Canadian tour on 8 October and were away for Charles's third birthday. Though the family were briefly reunited at Christmas, on 31 January 1952 further constitutional duties demanded that Princess Elizabeth and Prince Philip embark on a tour of British colonial Africa. They took care to telephone their two children – aged three and one – every day. Then, on 6 February 1952, while she and Philip were on safari in Kenya, Princess Elizabeth was summoned back to London upon the death of her father, King George VI, arriving the day after he had died. From that moment everything changed. The upbringing of Charles and Anne, previously little different from that of children in other aristocratic families, was never to be the same.

Prince Charles had always had more than one woman in his life: his mother, whom he looked up to and respected, and who ever since has remained on the pedestal on which he placed her as a child; his two nannies, whose love for him was unconditional and constant; and his grandmother, the Queen Mother. His nannies had a hands-on, affectionate relationship with him. He could do what he liked with them, and was – literally – the blue-eyed boy who could do no wrong. His relationship with his parents, while equally loving, was more formal. Given his status as heir to the throne, it was clearly understood that they were under an obligation to train him in his duties to his people and to his descendants.

As he grew up, his life became constricted by the demands of duty. He tried to please his father by agreeing to attend a school, Gordonstoun, suited more for SAS training than for that of a sensitive boy. He threw himself willingly into the world of horses, by which his father set great value, though in the early days at least he added to Prince Philip's disapproval by his inadequacies as a polo-player. By the time he had left Cambridge, in 1970, the dichotomy that was to dog his adult life had begun to be apparent. His concern for the welfare of his people and for his own spiritual well-being contrasted oddly with the violence and destruction of his passion for shooting and fox-hunting. His burgeoning interest in the inner self and in the welfare of those less fortunate developed at the same time as his passion for anthropology and archaeology. ('Digging up the past' may represent a wish to revisit his own past that had started off with promise in 1948 but which has not fulfilled its expectations.) He began to present a curious mixture of humanity and aggression – the latter, seldom expressed other than in field sports, perhaps being a reflection of his ambivalence towards the mother who loved him but then left him.

His entry into the real world – or one as real as it could be for a royal prince – was accompanied by mixed feelings towards women. On the one hand he was dependent upon their approval – as he depended and still does depend on the approval of his mother – and on the other he was attracted to the unconditional love of 'the other woman' or 'nanny'. Trapped between these two role models, Charles found himself in the unenviable position of being unable to make a commitment either to a holy Mary or to a harlot Mary Magdalen.

Prince Charles was introduced to several girls during the 1970s. None was a suitable candidate for marriage: their role was simply to allow him to 'sow his wild oats'. The result was more likely to have been a delay in settling down, since the unadventurous Charles must have found relations with 'unsuitable' partners more attractive than making a real commitment. Despite his great-uncle Lord Mountbatten's advice to have a fling when the opportunity offered, the often awkward and gauche Charles had difficulty in doing this in moderation, and Mountbatten on more than one occasion pointed out that he was in danger of following in the footsteps of his Uncle David (Edward VIII), as one woman after another was quickly taken up and just as quickly abandoned.

Charles needed reassurance that he was attractive to women. But he must often have wondered whether it was the image he projected of himself or the distant hope of marriage to a royal prince that attracted them to him. His external self-sufficiency had been instilled in him by Prince Philip, who had himself struggled with a fatherless childhood. The strength of Philip's character had helped him overcome life's disappointments, and his view was that Charles should do the same. That Charles was far more sensitive was not considered. It was not that Prince Philip was unaware of his son's feelings: he simply chose to ignore them. The aggressive comments for which he is notorious give some indication of the suppressed hostility within himself: 'British women can't cook' (1966), 'It looks as if it was put in by an Indian' (said while inspecting an unmodernized fusebox in a factory near Edinburgh in 1999) and 'You *are* a woman, aren't you?' (in Kenya in 1984, having accepted a token gift from a native woman). Amid calls to ban firearms after the massacre of children at Dunblane Primary School in 1996, he said, 'If a cricketer, for instance, suddenly decided to go into a school and batter a lot of people to death with a cricket bat, which he could do very easily, I mean, are you going to ban cricket bats?'

While it was true that many attractive women were only too pleased to have the heir to the throne as a consort, they soon realized that their relationship with Prince Charles had to do more with bolstering his sense of self-worth than with satisfying their marital expectations. The women by his side were often little more than fashion accessories – a statement to himself and to others that he was macho and therefore to be envied. Having been called 'Fatty' and 'Big Ears' at school, encouraged by his father to be a man when he had scarcely finished being a boy, and believing his brother Andrew to be better looking than he, it was hardly surprising that Charles had some catching up to do. He hid behind his royal status in order to to hide his shyness and self-consciousness, just as his great-grandfather George V had fallen back on the protection of his uniform. Under cover of the formality that he insisted upon from courtiers, Charles knew that he needed to grow up. But, struggling to become his own man rather than merely an extension of his father, he was not ready to abandon his youth for betrothal to a bride who, while satisfying the requirements of the House of Windsor, might not necessarily satisfy his own. The time would come soon enough when dynastic imperatives would take over. In the meantime the 1772 Royal Marriages Act would act as a protective umbrella, under cover of which he would be free to establish friendships with women – no matter how inappropriate – that would allow his long-suppressed emotions a free rein. It was clear to his parents that while his girlfriends boosted Charles's self-esteem they could never be suitable brides either because of their social standing or their marital status.

It was a couple of years after he had left Cambridge, in 1972, that Charles was formally introduced to the first of the two women who were to affect the course of his life. Though he had several affairs before his marriage to Lady Diana Spencer, it was only Camilla Parker Bowles, his later long-term mistress, and Princess Diana herself who were to have an indelible effect on him.

Camilla Parker Bowles was born in London in July 1947, the oldest of three children (two girls and a boy) of Major Bruce Shand, a well-known wine merchant and Deputy Lord Lieutenant of East Sussex. Camilla's mother, Rosalind Cubitt, was the daughter of Lord Ashcombe, whose forbears developed Belgravia. Camilla, as a daughter of a master of foxhounds, grew up against a background of hunting and other field sports. As Camilla Shand, she first met Charles, sixteen months her junior, in 1970 in a London nightclub, but she was not properly introduced to him until two years later, on a wet afternoon at Windsor Great Park, where the Prince was playing polo. She is reported to have said to him, 'I feel we have something in common. My great-great-grandmother [Alice Keppel] was your great-great-grandfather's [King Edward VII's] mistress, so how about it?' As an opening move it takes some beating, and the thirty-year game of chess that ensued must be the longest on record while she still waits for him to move his pawn.

Charles and Camilla spent a considerable amount of time together, and it is likely that he saw her as his missing other half. No intellectual, and not even particularly pretty, she nevertheless had charisma and was not so much good for a laugh as good for a 'chaff'. The apple-pie bed may be out of fashion, but the sense of humour it represents is still very much in as far as the royals are concerned, and discomfiting others is a royal tradition. Prince Philip is very good at it, and Camilla runs him a close second. On occasions such as Royal Ascot, she has been known to approach any man to whom she has taken a fancy and enquire of his partner, 'What are you doing with my boyfriend?'

Both Camilla and Charles were sent to schools entirely inappropriate to their future needs. Camilla's education began at fashionable Queensgate, where she was taught cookery and how to write cheques – dubious qualifications when the day came for her to marry a wealthy upper-class husband – and Charles was sent to the highly disciplined 'cold-baths-in-the-morning' Gordonstoun, which hardly prepared him for the psychological rigours of life in Buckingham Palace.

Charles and Camilla were clearly mutually attracted, and the Prince – whose self-esteem was low – was amazed by Camilla's interest in him. An immature 24-year-old, he was so stricken by her that soon after their introduction he confided to a friend that she was someone whom he would like one day to marry. Each saw in the other character traits which they themselves lacked. Camilla was an extrovert, whereas Charles was a moderately withdrawn, rather worried introvert. However, they also shared something to which couples who meet for the first time attach great value: they made each other laugh. Charles's attachment to the zany humour of the Goons reflected the fact that, as far as he was concerned, anything funny was good news, and Camilla was funny. Her sense of humour matched his own. When Charles married Princess Diana, nine years later, he discovered to his cost that she was not funny at all. If anything, she was depressed. He had never coped with his own depression, and he clearly was not able to cope with his wife's.

Until he met Camilla, Charles had found little to laugh about. His education at Gordonstoun and later at Cambridge had been a serious business at which he had struggled to make a success. His parents had been hard to please. As he got older, he must have wondered why his father had attended only two of his first eight birthdays – nine if one counted the day of his birth. He was eight years old when Prince Philip left for a five-month cruise on the royal yacht *Britannia* which led Ashley Wharton of the *Daily Express*, who wrote a series on the Queen's marriage, to report that 'there is a joke inside the family that Elizabeth would only know exactly where her husband was by checking the royal engagement listings in *The Times*'. Some questioned the stability of the relationship.

For the six months after their meeting, both Charles and Camilla were aware that a career in the Royal Navy was beckoning him. It is hard to believe that Prince Philip imagined his son as a sailor king who would follow in the footsteps of his great-grandfather King George V or, before him, of King William IV. It was more likely that he considered the Navy as an exercise in self-discipline and duty and an opportunity to acquire the social skills necessary for the diplomacy of kingship. Hierarchy was important to Prince Philip. He had had to climb the rungs of the royal ladder, and he saw no reason why his son should not at least go through the motions of climbing if not the royal ladder than at least the naval one.

In fact Prince Charles for the most part enjoyed his four years in the Navy, but he had great difficulty in coping with the technology of navigation and soon realized that life at sea was not for him. In December 1976, however, when the time came for his departure after more than one attempt to pass the examination in navigation technology, the senior officer of his squadron wrote that 'Prince Charles has attained an excellent level of professional competence as a Commanding Officer' and 'his manoeuvres have been a pleasure to witness'. Honour and tradition had now been satisfied. Charles had been popular with his shipmates, and had enjoyed the insistence on protocol between officers and men that was later to play an

important role in the pageantry and pomp of his own life. He had also taken
the opportunity for brief flirtations on shore leave which circumstances
occasionally allowed and which his father had instructed were to be encouraged by his mentors.

Once more on shore, Charles wondered what his next step should be. It
came as a great disappointment that, six months after he and Camilla Shand
had last met, she had accepted an offer of marriage from her old suitor, and
Charles's friend, the wealthy cavalry officer Colonel Andrew Parker Bowles.
There can be only two or three fairly obvious reasons why Camilla did not
wait for Charles. He may not have asked her to, leaving her in doubt about
his true feelings. She may have been in awe of his family and afraid that she
would be unable to play the role that a royal marriage would demand of her.
And, though her background was aristocratic, it may not have been as aristocratic as Prince Charles's family – and, in particular, Prince Philip – would
have liked.

Charles had in fact probably not thought of Camilla as a potential wife.
The first girlfriend about whom he was that serious was Lady Amanda
Knatchbull, granddaughter of his surrogate father, Lord Mountbatten. They
first met on the island of Eleuthera in 1973, when Amanda was fifteen and
Charles was ten years older. They saw each other increasing frequently over
the next few years, and in 1979 Charles broached the subject of marriage
with Amanda's mother, his godmother Lady Patricia Brabourne, who,
though considering Amanda to be suitable, felt that Charles was in too
much of a hurry to consider marriage. He was probably relieved by the
advice he was given, and it is likely that he had projected his own anxieties
about the pressures of royal family life on to Amanda when he told his great-
uncle that 'it would be a great sacrifice and loss of freedom' for her were he to
ask her to marry him. They remained good friends however, despite – or
more likely because of – her apparent reluctance to take on the enormous
responsibility that would befall her were she to go along with his marriage
plans.

All his other girlfriends were in many ways similar: blue-eyed blondes
with expectations. Unlike Amanda Knatchbull, they were willing to throw
in their lot with the good-looking but often sad and introspective Prince –

though one of them was immediately deemed unsuitable by the palace when it was discovered that she had previously loved another man. Charles was always careful to point out that marriage to the heir to the throne was no bed of roses and that there was a downside to what some women saw as a fairy-tale life. The 'duty' to which he constantly referred was a convenient defence against the fear of a commitment for which he was not ready. Those women who were slow to take the hint fell by the wayside.

Almost every woman with whom Charles had had a relationship before his marriage had regarded him as a Prince Charming who they might well have thought would bring romance, strength, security and emotional support to their lives. The responsibility for such expectations was often too much for him and, though Charles enjoyed the admiration and the sexual relationships that accompanied it, he would sometimes become so overwhelmed by the demands of the situation that he would literally run away. Hunting and fishing were not so much recreational activities as bolt-holes into which he could escape.

The turning point in Charles's life came in 1979, when Lord Louis Mountbatten was killed in an IRA bomb attack on his yacht *Shadow V* off the west coast of Ireland. Lady Patricia Brabourne was severely injured. Charles was devastated. Mountbatten had been everything to him, giving advice that, unlike that of others, who had various axes to grind, was neither sycophantic nor paternal – though in hindsight it was often inappropriate. The Prince had shared feelings with him that he could share with no one else. He had lost his best friend. Mountbatten, though far older, had always respected his nephew's views and had discussed with him both personal and other issues.

Charles had 'lost' his biological parents to their constitutional duties at the age of three, and now he had lost his surrogate parent. It was time to address his destiny. Within two years of the terrorist attack on Mountbatten, Charles proposed marriage to Lady Diana Spencer. Twelve years younger than Charles, Diana was a direct descendant of King Charles II, a continuity all the more poignant because, when the time came for Charles to succeed his mother, he would take the title of King Charles III.

Up to and during his marriage to Diana, Charles had so-called 'confidantes' rather than mistresses. This appellation was acceptable not only because it explained his failure to make a commitment, but also because it had more acceptable overtones. He did his best to confront his fear of intimacy by marrying Diana, but there remained too many windows of escape from what he most feared, and the marriage was therefore ultimately unsuccessful. Much has been written about the reasons for the breakdown, ranging from his inability to cope with Diana's psychological problems and her inability to cope with his, to the existence of Charles's 'confidantes' who from time to time intervened. Though others did in fact come between them, the shadows were more likely to have been cast by significant inhabitants of their childhoods.

When Prince Charles looked at the frail and psychologically damaged girl by his side in Westminster Abbey on his wedding-day in 1981, he might have wondered if she would ever be able to compensate him for what his childhood had denied him. As children, both Charles and Diana were given intimacy only to have it snatched away from them – in Charles's case by the death of his grandfather and the subsequent unavailability of his parents and in Diana's by her parents' divorce – so it was inevitable that neither would grow up with a strong sense of self-worth. No child can be expected to cope with the turning away of parents when they are most needed. Both Charles and Diana were angry. Diana expressed her anger by using body language – throwing back the 'feeds' of infancy into the face of a mother who had fed her and left her – and Charles expressed his by being unable to tolerate courtiers turning their backs on him as they left his presence.

Charles's emotional needs were no different from Diana's, but they were expressed more subtly. When their marriage began to crumble, Diana at first sought to compensate for her low sense of self-worth by gaining admiration through her acquisition of a striking visual image and the lifestyle that went with it. Charles, for his part, sought the wisdom of older men. He had lost his great-uncle Lord Mountbatten and had come to rely on the writer and explorer Laurens Van der Post. It was only many years later that the writer J.D.F. Jones revealed that Charles's hero – a war hero and a supposed authority on the work of the psychoanalyst Carl Gustav Jung and the Bushmen of the Kalahari Desert – was also a multiple adulterer. As well as deceiving at least two of his mistresses with much younger women, when he was seventy-eight he seduced a reluctant twenty-three-year-old girl in his hotel bedroom in Cape Town, after telling her that she was his muse. The girl described the incident as a 'rape'.

Apart from Laurens Van der Post, after the death of Lord Mountbatten there was no one with whom Charles could share his innermost thoughts except Camilla Parker Bowles.

Camilla was one of Prince Charles's first confidantes. He had even sought her help in finding his future queen. Charles understood the nature of the role she was expected to play in his life better than she did. It was a role that necessarily required discretion and mutual trust, and it was one which had hitherto been played by Kurt Hahn, his headmaster at Gordonstoun, and by Lord Mountbatten and which was now shared with Laurens Van der Post. His interactions with these surrogate fathers mimicked the intimacy between client and therapist. Camilla was the first woman to undertake the role hitherto played by his male mentors. If sexual contact had occurred with Camilla at the time in the early 1970s when she became his confidante, it would thus have been as between therapist and client – incestuous, incongruent and forbidden. It is therefore unlikely that it took place, and it would thus have been with a clear conscience that Camilla had married Andrew Parker Bowles.

From the moment of birth, the relationship between child and mother is one that depends on an intimacy of physical contact, an absoluteness of dependency, an acceptance of vulnerability and a totality of trust. Later it is repeated between child and father. Had the immature Charles married Camilla at this very early dependent stage in their relationship, the marriage might well have been as one between mentor and analysand and would have had to accommodate the ambivalence of the first relationship of all: the absolute love of the infant for his mother when all goes well but also the absolute hate for her when it does not. Such a marriage would most likely have failed when their dependent need for one another faded. That the quasi-therapeutic boundaries that separated Charles and Camilla early in their relationship were eventually breached, to be replaced by genuine passion, is unequivocally suggested by the telephone conversation eavesdropped on on 18 December 1989 and famously known as 'Camillagate'. Three years before Charles separated from Diana, Charles and Camilla discussed in the vernacular, as only lovers would, the urgency of their passion, both erotic and affectionate, for one another. Their breathless six-minute bedroom conversation was circulated at first in Australia, then in Europe and finally in 1993 in the *Sunday Mirror* and the *Sunday People* in the UK.

Camilla would not have been the first royal mistress to believe that her interests would be better served in an ongoing affair without responsibility. She has been all things to Charles. As well as being his confidante and playmate, she has lifted his spirits and allowed him the freedom to walk in and out of her life at will. Camilla was the antithesis of the shy Diana. Never at a loss for a word and bubbling over with energy and enthusiasm, she has kept a low profile and always been there for him. Emotionally, no royal duties have separated them.

Charles's background is one of commitment avoided. Long before Diana's tragic death in a road-traffic accident in Paris in 1997, he found that commitment did not work for him. He has not always been faithful to his confidantes – and how could he be, when his emotional needs were not fulfilled from when he was three years old? His parents' commitment was interrupted far too often for him to have much faith in subsequent involvements.

Charles has been quoted as saying that Dale, Lady Tryon – 'Kanga', the Australian dress designer – is 'the only woman who really understands me'. The fact that he feels he needs to be 'understood' at all says more about Charles than about the women he has been close to. All of them, Amanda, Camilla, Kanga, Diana, were ultimately unavailable. Camilla married soon after they first met; Kanga was married to Lord Tryon, one of his oldest friends and later godfather to Prince William; Amanda was too young at the time; and he married Diana before he was ready to do so.

The Prince of Wales is familiar with his family history. He has no need to emulate the buffoonery of a William IV, to involve himself in the relentless pursuit of virility like Henry VIII or to become a sex addict like Charles II, whose insatiable needs drove him into the arms of one woman after another. Prince Charles wants to lead a normal life, to create a home for himself and his family from which his doubts about self-worth will be expunged. Diana eventually overcame her bulimia through her acceptance of the love of all who knew her. But, more than four years into widowhood, Charles's fear of rejection continues to trouble him to the extent that, given the opportunity to remarry and relinquish his inheritance in favour of his elder son, he continues to prevaricate.

By 2002 Charles and Camilla had known each other for more than thirty years, during the last six of which they have both been divorced; yet a marriage between them has still not materialized. Camilla's gift to Charles before his wedding to Diana was a pair of cufflinks inscribed with two intertwined Cs – golden handcuffs which he wore even on his honeymoon. Their nicknames for each other are Fred and Gladys, characters from a 1950s radio comedy. Are they still trapped in the past, ongoing characters in a royal *Goon Show*, or are they now sufficiently self-confident to be able to replace the cufflinks with a wedding-band?

Select Bibliography

Airey, Osmund, *Charles II* (London: Longmans Green and Co., 1904)

Allen, Walter Gore, *King William IV* (London: Cresset Press, 1960)

Amory, Cleveland, *Who Killed Society?* (New York: Harper and Brothers, 1960)

Aronson, Theo, *The King in Love* (London: John Murray, 1988)

Ashley, Maurice, *James II* (London: Hamish Hamilton, 1972)

Asquith, Cynthia, *Lady Cynthia Asquith Diaries 1915–1918* (London: Hutchinson, 1968)

Balsan, Consuelo Vanderbilt, *The Glitter and the Gold* (New York: Harper Brothers, 1952)

Beaton, Cecil, *The Wandering Years* (Boston: Little, Brown, 1961)

Bloch, Michael (ed.), *Wallis and Edward, Letters 1931–1937: The Intimate Correspondence of the Duke and Duchess of Windsor* (London. Weidenfeld and Nicolson, 1986)

——, *The Secret File of the Duke of Windsor* (London: Bantam Press, 1988)

——, *The Duchess of Windsor* (London: Weidenfeld & Nicolson, 1996)

——, *The Reign and Abdication of Edward VIII* (London: Bantam, 1990)

Blunden, Margaret, *The Countess of Warwick* (London: Cassell, 1967)

Bocca, Geoffrey, *She Might Have Been Queen* (London: Express Books, 1955)

Brandon, Ruth, *Being Divine* (London: Secker & Warburg, 1991)

Bryan, J. III, and Charles J.V. Murphy., *The Windsor Story* (London: Granada, 1979)

Campbell, Lady Colin, *The Royal Marriages* (New York: Smith Gryphon, 1993)

Cartland, Barbara, *Romantic Royal Marriages* (London: Express Books, 1981)

Chambers Biographical Dictionary, 6th edn (Edinburgh: Chambers, 1997)

Channon, Sir Henry, *The Diaries of Henry Channon*, ed. Robert Rhodes James (London: Weidenfeld and Nicolson, 1967)

Delderfield, Eric, *Kings and Queens of England and Great Britain* (Newton Abbott: David and Charles, 1971)

Donaldson, Frances, *Edward VIII* (London: Weidenfeld and Nicolson, 1974)

Edwards, Ann, *Matriarch: Queen Mary and the House of Windsor* (London: Hodder and Stoughton, 1984)

Ellmann, Richard, *Oscar Wilde* (Harmondsworth: Penguin, 1988)

Fairclough, Melvyn, *The Ripper and the Royals* (London: Duckworth, 1991)

Fea, Alan, *James II and His Wives* (London: Methuen, 1908)

Fraser, Antonia (ed.), *The Lives of the Kings and Queens of England* (London: Weidenfeld and Nicolson, 1975)

——, *The Six Wives of Henry VIII* (London: Weidenfeld and Nicolson, 1992)

Friedman, Rosemary, *A Loving Mistress* (London: House of Stratus, 2001)

Gerson, Noel B., *Lily Langtry: A Biography* (London: Robert Hale, 1972)

Glyn, Sir Anthony, *Elinor Glyn* (London: Hutchinson, 1955)

Godfrey, Rupert (ed.), *Letters from a Prince: Edward, Prince of Wales to Mrs Frieda Dudley Ward, March 1918 – January 1921* (London: Little, Brown, 1998)

Goldsmith, Barbara, *Little Gloria . . . Happy at Last* (New York: Knopf, 1980)

Hamilton, Lord Ernest, *The Halcyon Era* (London: John Murray, 1933)

Hardy, Alan, *The King's Mistresses* (London: Evans Brothers, 1980)

Hibbert, Christopher, *Edward VII* (London: Allen Lane, 1976)

Higham, Charles, *The Duchess of Windsor: The Secret Life* (New York: McGraw-Hill, 1988)

——, *Merle Oberon* (London: New English Library, 1983)

Higham, F.M.G., *King James II* (London: Hamish Hamilton, 1934)

Hilliam, David, *Kings, Queens, Bones and Bastards: Who's Who in the English Monarchy from Egbert to Elizabeth II* (Stroud: Sutton, 1998)

Hillsdon, Sonia, *The Jersey Lily* (Guernsey: Seaflower Books, 1993)

Holden, Anthony, *Prince Charles* (London: Weidenfeld and Nicolson, 1979)

Howarth, Patrick, *George VI* (London: Hutchinson, 1987)

Jerrold, Walter, *Henry VIII and His Wives* (London: Hutchinson, 1933)

Jones, J.D.F., *Storyteller: The Many Lives of Laurens Van der Post* (London: John Murray, 2001)

Julian, Philippe, *Edward and the Edwardians* (London: Sidgwick and Jackson, 1967)

Keppel, Sonia, *Edwardian Daughter* (London: Hamish Hamilton, 1958)

King, Greg, *The Duchess of Windsor* (London: Aurum Press, 1999)

Lee, Christopher, *This Sceptred Isle 55 BC–1901* (Harmondsworth and London: Penguin Books and BBC Books, 1997)

Lee, Sir Sydney, *King Edward VII: A Biography* (London: Macmillan, 2 vols., 1925, 1927)

Leslie, Anita, *Edwardians in Love* (London: Hutchinson, 1972)

Lockridge, Norman, *Lese Majesty: The Private Lives of the Duke and Duchess of Windsor* (New York: Boar's Head Books, 1952)

Longford, Elizabeth (ed.), *The Oxford Book of Royal Anecdotes* (Oxford and New York: Oxford University Press, 1989)

Longueville, T., *The Adventures of King James of England* (London, New York and Bombay: Longmans, Green and Co., 1904)

McLeod, Kirsty, *Battle Royal: Edward VIII and George VI, Brother against Brother* (London: Constable, 1999)

Magnus, Sir Philip, *King Edward VII* (London: John Murray, 1964)

—— (ed.), *Queen Victoria's Letters* (London: Penguin, 1964)

Martin, Ralph G., *The Woman He Loved* (New York: Simon and Schuster, 1973)

Masters, Brian, *The Mistresses of Charles II* (London: Blond and Briggs, 1979)

Menzies, Amy, *Further Indiscretions* (London: Herbert Jenkins, 1918)

Mumby, F.A., *The Youth of Henry VIII: A Narrative in Contemporary Letters* (London: Constable, 1913)

Pearson, Hesketh, *The Life of Oscar Wilde* (London: Methuen, 1946)

Pepys, Samuel, *The Diary of Samuel Pepys*, ed. Robert Latham and William Matthews (London: G. Bell and Sons, 1970)

Pocock, Tom, *Sailor King* (London: Sinclair-Stephenson, 1991)

Pope-Hennessy, James, *Queen Mary* (London: Allen and Unwin, 1959)

Ridley, Jasper, *Henry VIII* (London: Constable, 1984)

St Aubyn, Giles, *Edward VII, Prince and King* (London: Collins, 1979)

St John, Adela Rogers, *The Honeycomb* (New York: Doubleday, 1969)

Scott, J. W. Robertson, *The Life and Death of a Newspaper: An Account of the Temperaments, Perturbations and Achievements of John Morley, W.T. Stead . . . and . . . Other Editors of the Pall Mall Gazette* (London: Methuen, 1952)

Somerset, Anne, *The Life and Times of William IV* (London: Weidenfeld and Nicolson, 1980)

Stone, Lawrence, *The Family, Sex and Marriage in England 1500–1800* (Harmondsworth: Penguin, 1977)

Thornton, Michael, *Royal Feud* (London: Michael Joseph, 1985)

Tomalin, Claire, *Mrs Jordan's Profession* (London: Viking, 1994)

Trefusis, Violet, *Don't Look Back* (London: Hutchinson, 1952)

Turner, F. C., *James II* (London: Eyre and Spottiswoode, 1948)

Vanderbilt, Gloria, and Thelma, Lady Furness , *Double Exposure: A Twin Autobiography* (New York: David McKay, 1958)

Vreeland, Diana, *DV* (New York: Knopf, 1984)

Warwick, Christopher, *Abdication* (London: Sidgwick and Jackson, 1986)

Weir, Alison, *The Six Wives of Henry VIII* (London: Bodley Head, 1991)

——, *Henry VIII, King and Court* (London: Jonathan Cape, 2001)

Williamson, David, *Kings and Queens of England* (London: National Portrait Gallery, 1998)

Wilson, Christopher, *Dancing with the Devil* (London: HarperCollins, 2000)

Windsor, The Duchess of, *The Heart Has Its Reasons* (London: Michael Joseph, 1956)

Windsor, HRH the Duke of, *A King's Story* (London: Cassell, 1951)

Wycherley, William, *The Country Wife*, ed. Thomas H. Fugimura (Omaha: University of Nebraska Press, 1965)

Ziegler, Philip, *King Edward VIII* (London: Collins, 1990)

Index

women, 179–80; character and
values, 179, 181–2; relations with
Pamela Parker Bowles, 181–4, 187–9;
naval career, 183; romances and girl
friends, 184–5, 188; relations with
Mountbatten, 185–6; emotional
needs, 186, 188–9
Charlotte, Queen of George III, 79–81,
85, 92
Chesterfield, Elizabeth, Countess of
(*née* Butler), 71
Chesterfield, Philip Dormer Stanhope,
2nd Earl of, 47–8, 71, 74
children: beatings, 130
Christian IX, King of Denmark, 99
Christina, Duchess of Milan, 37
Churchill, Lady Arabella (*later*
Godfrey), 72–5
Churchill, John *see* Marlborough, 1st
Duke of
Churchill, Sir Winston, 165
Ciano, Count Galeazzo, 155
Civil War (English), 43–4
Clarence, Prince Albert, Duke of
('Eddy'), 125–7
Clarendon, Edward Hyde, 1st Earl of,
46, 50–1, 69, 71
Clement VII, Pope, 31–2
Clifden, Nellie, 98–9
Clinton, Bill, 14, 160
Clinton, Edward Fiennes de, 9th
Baron, 28
Coates, Audrey (*née* James), 141
Coates, Major Dudley, 141

Cobbett, William, 91
Coke, Marion, Viscountess (*née*
Trefusis), 134–5
Coke, Thomas William, Viscount, 134
Colyear, Sir David (*later* Earl of
Portmore), 76
Compton, Sir William, 24, 35
Conroy, Sir John, 95–6
Converse, James Vail ('Junior'), 142–4
Cooper, Lady Diana, 162
Cooper, Gary, 168
Cordet, Hélène, 177
corporal punishment, 130
Coward, Noël, 170
Cranmer, Thomas, Archbishop of
Canterbury, 31
Cromwell, Oliver, 44, 46, 58
Cromwell, Thomas (*later* Earl of
Essex), 31, 33
Crook, Annie, 126
Cruikshank, George, 91
Culpepper, Thomas, 39
Cumberland, Prince Ernest Augustus,
Duke of, 80

Dalton, Revd John, 125
Daly, Richard, 89
Darnley, James, 75
Davis, Mary, 52
Dawson, Geoffrey, 165
Dawson of Penn, Bertrand Edward,
Viscount, 160
Delamere, Gladys, Lady, 142
Denham, Sir John, 71–2